Earthing The Dragon

Glastonbury and the 60s

ADAM STOUT

GREEN MAGIC

Green Magic
53 Brooks Road
Street
Somerset
BA16 0PP
England
www.greenmagicpublishing.com

Designed and typeset by Carrigboy, Wells, UK
www.carrigboy.co.uk

ISBN 978 1 915580 28 3

GREEN MAGIC

Contents

Acknowledgements

BIG THANKS for help, advice, interviews, proofreading and permissions to Richard Adams, Jo Berryman, Adrian Blamires, Scorpio Bickerstaffe, the British Library, Bristol University Library, Philip Carr-Gomm, the Chalice Well Trustees, Francis Deas, Alison Dhuanna, the Findhorn Foundation Trustees, Paul Fletcher, Bruce Garrard, Glastonbury Town Council, Stewart Harding, Carmen Hesketh, Tim Hill, the John Michell Archive, Nicola Keene, Yuri Leitch, Liz Leyshon, Anthony Mawson, Charles Michell, Barry Miles, Gareth Mills, Paul Misso, Muz Murray, Jan Oakley, Christine Rhone, Serena Roney-Dougal, Gina Schiraldi, Paul Screeton, Terry Maine, the Victoria and Albert Museum, Angie Watts and Andy White, with a special mention to Paul Weston for oblique inspiration. Any defects, mistakes or misconceptions are entirely the fault of the dragons.

Introduction

"Most people who get close to Glastonbury seem to go mad, more or less. Sometimes with the higher madness which is wisdom; sometimes not. The professional scholars (with a few exceptions) get as unbalanced as anybody else; only they are cleverer at appearing to be sane." Thus spake Geoffrey Ashe, surrendering his sanity to the mauve pages of *Gandalf's Garden* in his 1969 appeal to the people to join "the enduring community of Avalon." What follows is my own meander through the colourful years that shaped the modern Glastonbury phenomenon, both town and festival, and perhaps the wider world as well. It's not an in-depth scholarly analysis but a sketch, a snapshot with only moderate resolution, intentionally not over-researched, although I am fanatical about chronology. One thing leads to another. Finding the sequence of events is the best way to understand how this strange flower came to blossom. This screed is an appraisal of the ideas, elements, catalysts and players that made it happen; neither endorsing nor criticising them, simply trying to understand them. It's a tale of two Merlins and a Gandalf, of upper class and underclass, of gilded hippies and LSD, of dragon-lines and earth energies, dreamers and activists, of fashion high and low, colour in the grey, the little town in the heart of the land, the cosmopolitan city, rough and glittering, and LSD, and King Arthur, whoever he was, and St. Michael, and the New Age, and Catholics and mystics and LSD and flying saucers and sacred geometry and the quest, sorry, Quest, for meaning, spiritual, national, eternal.

There's a little bit of background, but hopefully not too much; Patrick Benham's *The Avalonians* is still the best guide to the previous round of Glastonbury mystics and Bruce Garrard's *Free State* is an engaging and fulsome account of the struggles and successes of the 'New Glastonbury Community' that began to settle in numbers after 1971, when the history part of my book stops. I've similarly truncated the future careers of all the major players, to keep the focus tight, the pagination down and the readership interested. As Kurt Vonnegut said, a book should start as close to the end as possible.

The Mad King's Road

I turned eight during the Summer of Love of 1967. I started a new school that September, and every morning I caught the No. 11 along the King's Road, dutifully clutching my fourpenny-half to the Worlds End, an exotic destination if ever there was one. The outward journey was fast enough – what self-respecting hippy was ever up at half past eight? – but in the afternoons the street was packed with colourful people, some of them barefoot, slowing down my homebound bus and keeping me from my toast soldiers. I remember being mildly scandalised by the giant – is it? – no it can't be, surely, it is! – boob painted on a window shutter. The shops were bright, wild and weird, and the closer you got to the World's End, the weirder the shops became, appropriately enough. At the World's End itself was the most flamboyant shop of all, Granny Takes A Trip, which at one point featured the front of an American car sticking out from the facade. It was all very exciting.

Everyone and everything seemed larger than life and the colours twice as bright as elsewhere, and the main reason for that, unbeknownst to little me, was the wildfire spread of the miracle drug LSD amongst Chelsea's *haut hipoisie* (a term devised by that wordsmith Marianne Faithfull for the tribe she herself belonged to), and their myriad admirers, customers and acolytes. The scene began a year earlier: "There were the strains of a prolonged party in the air," recalled socialite and bon vivant Henrietta Moraes.

> *I heard them faintly at first. 'I say, there's an extraordinary new thing about, it's called acid. It's not exactly a drug. Anyway, you take it on a sugar cube and go to heaven or something.' There was a new look on the streets. Long-silky-haired youths and girls dressed in silks, satins, ribbons and laces, gentle smiles on radiant faces, festoons of flowers. One saw a sort of esoteric kind of camaraderie … Almost everyone of my circle downed tools, if ever they'd taken them up, and abandoned work …*

They made the drug illegal at the end of 1966, which of course made it a hundred times more attractive to the rebel generation, whether they actually took it or not. The 'contact high' was a real phenomenon. Joy can be contagious. Shawn Levy described the Chelsea scene as "a general, if benign, madness, a kind of communicable derangement of the senses."

But acid was more than just about making you feel good. It made you question absolutely everything that previous generations had taken for granted. Outside the bubble, the Vietnam War ground on, the Soviet Union was invading its allies, and Britain was floundering to find a place for itself in a polarised world. LSD's transformational properties were first discovered in 1943, the same year in which work began on the atom bomb. Many saw acid and the revelations it encouraged as an antidote to atomic weapons, salvation for a shameful species. It was part of the toolbox of the new Aquarian Age. Antique dealer and Chelsea fashion-broker Christopher Gibbs remembered those days as

> a time of experiment, dope-fuelled and acid-elevated, when, questioning everything, loosening all sorts of anchors, we sought enlightenment, liberty from the weight of received opinion, escape from Vanity Fair, a glimpse of the plains of heaven. I had little money, but I was fascinated by all I was learning ... delighted by the parade of punters that I seemed to attract, earning just enough to live the life that pleased me. It was a time of change, of mass illumination through music, drugs, and a crumbling of worn-out certainties.

The Chelsea crowd looked west for inspiration. According to Barry Miles, co-founder of the underground magazine *International Times* and a convincing guide to the swinging city, they were endlessly discussing flying saucers, ley lines and the court of King Arthur, reading Geoffrey Ashe and John Michell, learning about magic and the Old Ways. "It was an important side of the English underground scene, informing the posters, the graphic art, the song lyrics and the poetry; it had no counterpart in the USA, except for the pioneer tradition." At the heart of it all was Glastonbury. Like a mighty ley line, "the King's Road led straight to Glastonbury in those days."

CHAPTER ONE

Jerusalemic Britain

GLASTONBURY TAMED

To understand how all this came about, we must backtrack a bit. Glastonbury, a small town in Somerset that grew up around an important abbey, had enjoyed (or endured, depending on your point of view) a wondrously mystical reputation since the Middle Ages. King Arthur was said to have been buried there, and after Henry VIII's destruction of the Abbey, a miraculous thorn tree survived that flowered in midwinter, some said on Christmas Day. Over time, the story grew that the tree had sprung from the staff of Joseph of Arimathea, legendary founder of Glastonbury, who had arrived in Britain centuries before the Catholic Church had been established. This not only confirmed the national conviction that Britain had been specially selected and blessed by God, but also conferred spiritual supremacy for the British brand of Christianity.

The town became a kind of capital of anti-rationalism in the mid-eighteenth century, when an asthmatic farmer was cured of his malaise on the advice of a Voice that told him to drink water from a horse trough by the Chain Gate for seven Sundays in a row. This water came from a stream that started at the Chalice Well and ran across the Abbey grounds, acquiring healing qualities from the bones of all the saints and martyrs buried there, and thousands of people flocked to Glastonbury to be cured, or otherwise. A century later, as the Industrial Revolution cranked into high gear and much of the land became sullied and grimed, some came to see Glastonbury, deep in the green heartlands, as the place where England kept its soul, and the town's reputation grew steadily more mystical.

Tennyson's epic Arthurian poem *Idylls of the King* brought the Holy Grail to Glastonbury in 1869; in 1886 Alice Meadows, niece of the proprietor of the Chalice Well, claimed that Christ himself had buried the Grail beneath Chalice Hill, in a poem which may have clinched the sale with the Catholic Confraternity of the Sacred Heart who bought the Well that year. A decade later, one Dr. John Goodchild, a psychic and Celticist much caught up with the Celtic revival, buried a vessel that came to be called the Blue Bowl in a well at the other end of town, near the chapel at Beckery which had been dedicated to the fifth-century Irish saint Bride. He did this in response to a waking dream in which a voice (another one: the Isle of Avalon is full of voices) told him that this vessel had once been carried by Jesus, that it had a powerful influence to play in shaping the thought of the twentieth century, and that he should take it to Glastonbury and 'place it in the Women's Quarter' there, for a maiden to retrieve at a later date. The Blue Bowl was duly discovered seven years later by three young women from Bristol, one of whom had a brother called Wellesley Tudor Pole who had also had a powerful dream about Glastonbury, which convinced him that the Chalice Well had an important role to play in its future. In 1907 Tudor Pole, TP to his friends, took the Blue Bowl to various experts for appraisal, including senior churchmen. The ruins of Glastonbury Abbey had just been bought on behalf of the Church of England, and the heady atmosphere may help to explain why this twenty-three-year-old found such an attentive audience amongst the great-and-good for his "very strong intuition" that "Glastonbury will become the centre of healing as at Lourdes, a centre not only of physical but also of spiritual healing." The finding of the Blue Bowl meant that "through Glastonbury is Christianity to be renewed here in England." Archdeacon Wilberforce believed that it was the Holy Grail, or so he told Mark Twain.

I've singled out TP because he returned to Glastonbury at the end of his days and helped to shape the form the mythos takes today, but many other mystics and eccentrics came to Glastonbury during the following decades. Patrick Benham dubbed them 'the Avalonians' in his pioneering book, and I won't go into any detail here but will just mention briefly the ones whose work had clear resonance with the people who came in the 60s. There was Frederick Bligh Bond, conscientious archaeologist at Glastonbury Abbey for many years until the revelation that he'd been guided in his work by a long-dead monk led the authorities to ease him out; Dion Fortune, novelist and mystic who straddled the boundary between Christianity and Paganism; Katherine Maltwood, who in 1934 published an account of a giant prehistoric zodiac she perceived in the landscape around the town, which she called 'the Temple of the Stars'; and Lionel Smithett Lewis, vicar from 1922 to 1951, who was convinced that not only Joseph of Arimathea but Christ himself had come to visit Glastonbury, and shared his ideas with an enthusiastic following through several editions of his book.

But by the 1960s, all these characters were long gone. The Winds of Truth still blew around Elsie Hartshorn's Sanctuary of the Silver Lily on Ashwell Lane, though they were little more than a slight breeze now, and unknown to the uninitiated. Other spiritual eccentrics were dotted around, and visitors came on esoteric missions of their own, but their impact on the life of the town was minimal. A Glastonbury Thorn was planted on Wirral Hill in 1951, and the annual tradition of sending a cutting to the monarch at Christmas became institutionalised, but this was tame stuff compared to the baroque ideas of the Avalonians. Louis MacNeice, coming here for the first time in 1953, found the Abbey ruins "green and muted." The Fifties was a pretty soulless decade in general, in truth. Science was triumphant and salvation was brewed in test tubes. The country was recovering from wartime austerity, consumer spending was on the up, and people were heads-down wallowing, never having had it so good … Just so long as they didn't think too much about the shadow of nuclear annihilation and the Cold War, or the rapid dismantling of the British Empire in a world where Britain no longer called the shots.

ARTHUR RETURNS

In this rational decade, it took the Catholics, with their commitment to ritual and mystery, to keep the flame of romance burning. Eighteen thousand of them came to Glastonbury in 1955 to witness the return of the shrine of Our Lady, and hear a bishop take the Protestants to task for banishing the comforting cult of Mary: "The fierce invective of the Old Testament came more easily to men's lips than the pity and chivalry of Medieval times." Seen in this context, the very Catholic Meriol Trevor's novel *The Last of Britain* seems almost allegorical. It was published in 1956, the year of Suez when Britain's inability to operate alone on the world stage became humiliatingly clear, and was set in the Dark Ages at the precise moment when the British were defeated by the Saxons. The hero takes solace in faith:

> *The rise and fall of nations was nothing to the redeemer and ruler of all nations. Perhaps the Britons suffered now for the follies and pride of the time of their prosperity; perhaps God would draw from their anguish some new glory. But what mattered was to*

serve him, in whatever time, whether of sorrow or more dangerous ease … Bowing down to the frosty earth, Theo heard the divine voice, speaking in his heart, speaking in mercy and triumph: "I am Lord of the Defeated."

The hero is a novice at Glastonbury Abbey, and Glastonbury is at the heart of Trevor's story. It is "the holy place of Britain," "Jerusalem in Britain," and "the holy place where there is always peace," "the secret and holy island of Avalon," the last retreat of the last British survivors. It was the place where the story should have ended – but at least one reader drew the opposite conclusion. "The atmosphere is too futile and negative, the effect is too wan," declared Geoffrey Ashe, "but the striking thing about the book is that it should have been written. It marked the trend, and it acted as a stimulus" – a stimulus to himself in particular, since the following year he published *King Arthur's Avalon*. Wildly successful, his book was the complete antidote to *The Last of Britain*. It was all about beginnings, not endings, and it invoked the mystery of King Arthur in the cause.

Geoffrey Ashe's influence in shaping the modern mythos of Glastonbury was enormous. Born in 1923, he, like Trevor, was a devout Catholic and was first drawn to Glastonbury when he read Christopher Hollis' fiery polemic of 1927, *Glastonbury and England* ("History is either Catholic or anti-Catholic. The impartial historian is simply an atheist without the

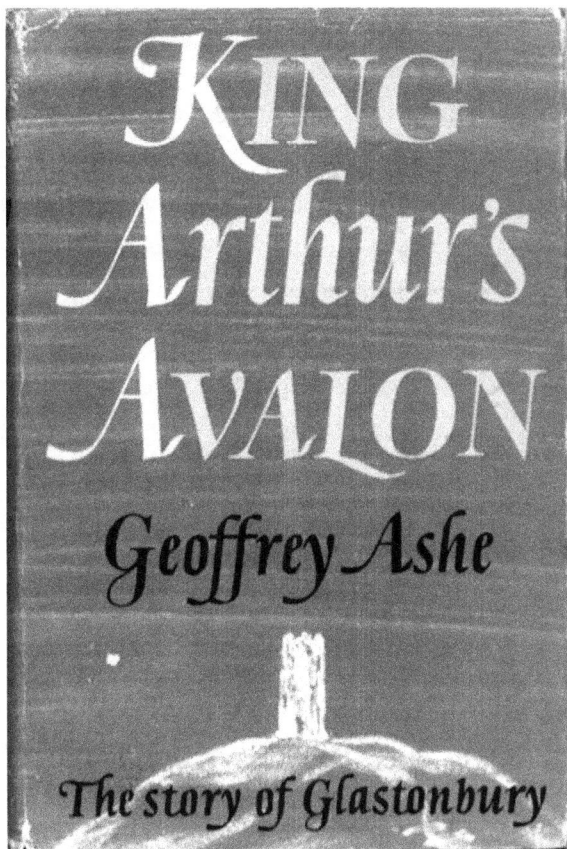

courage of his convictions" – now that's telling us), which concluded with a probably-spurious claim made by the last monk of Glastonbury that the Abbey would one day be repaired and rebuilt. "The words hit me with the force of a revelation," wrote Ashe. "They gave me my orders. Glastonbury was going to be reborn and that was what I had to work for. Since writing was my only talent, the first step for me to take was to write a book about Glastonbury. I returned to England, visited the place, and sold the idea of a book to Collins"…

Without Arthur's name in the title, it is doubtful that the book would have caught the public eye. The idea of Arthur, the romantic, elusive king-under-the-mountain, ready to arise and rescue the country at its hour of deepest need, was very appealing in those unsettling years, in which well-disposed folk were conjuring up better futures from the legendary past. 1958 saw the republication of T.H. White's classic Arthurian trilogy as *The Once and Future King* – with an extra final book, *The Candle in the Wind*, in which the dying king dreams of a future without wars and without countries. In the same year, Jack Lindsay's *Arthur and his Times* appeared: the author, a communist, concludes by praising the Celts for creating "a universal champion, a hero slumbering in the hearts of the people still awoken by the trumpet of freedom." Ashe's work lay somewhere in between the two; it is a compelling and engagingly-written account in which the reader is left in little doubt that the author believes there once was a historical king. The surprising thing is just how small a proportion of the book is actually devoted to him at all. The book is about Avalon much more than it is about Arthur, and as he says in his preface to the second edition:

> *I wrote under the spell of a conviction: that Glastonbury, England's New Jerusalem, is strong magic and not dead merely because its Abbey is ruined. That conviction has never deserted me. Whatever the nature of the magic, it is there and*

it will revive. The future is greater than the past. My aim was (and is) not antiquarian study for its own sake but the rebirth of Glastonbury with all it implies; and my motive in undertaking a book was partly to make the holy place better known, partly to define what it was and what it did imply.

King Arthur's Avalon is a well-disguised polemic, in which restitution of Glastonbury to the Catholic fold is central, but not overt; and it is curious that another devout Catholic, J.R.R. Tolkien, managed to play down his faith in much the same way and at much the same time in the pages of *The Lord of the Rings* (published in 1954–55). There is a study to be written on the place of Catholicism in the re-enchantment of Britain. Tolkien's intention, as he claimed, was "to restore to the English an epic tradition and present them with a mythology of their own," and it's possibly no coincidence that many of the first generation of Glastonbury's hippy settlers came from Catholic backgrounds, or that all of them were steeped in the work of Ashe and Tolkien.

Interest in Arthur continued unabated during the 1960s. The archaeologist Ralegh Radford, engaged in long-term excavations at Glastonbury Abbey, in 1962–3 diverted his energies into looking for Arthur's grave, and convinced himself that he had succeeded (the fact that later archaeologists were less convinced is beside the point). Fuelled and inspired by this renewed interest, the Camelot Research Committee was set up, with Radford as chair and Ashe as the secretary, to raise money to excavate the hillfort of Cadbury Castle, twelve miles from Glastonbury, which the sixteenth-century antiquarian John Leland had claimed had been the site of the original Camelot. The excavations, led by Leslie Alcock, spanned five seasons between 1966 and 1970, and the dig attracted a huge amount of attention. 5000 people visited the site during 1967 alone; that year's Bath Festival adopted an Arthurian theme, with an open-air pageant held beside the Abbey Church, lectures by Alcock and Ashe, and guided coach expeditions to Cadbury and Glastonbury.

Perhaps the publicity highpoint of the whole exercise was the appearance of the lavishly-published *The Quest for Arthur's Britain* in 1968. Edited by Ashe, it featured contributions by several important archaeologists, but it was Ashe that pulled it together and drew the conclusions. In the final chapter, titled 'The New Matter of Britain,' he suggested that contemporary interest in Arthur could be seen as a kind of national renewal:

> *To live with the Arthurian theme for long is to feel that the prophecy of Arthur's Return means something, though it may be hard to say what. An answer, possibly, has now begun to take shape. As the exploration of national roots goes on, there are signs in Britain of a new disposition to ask, 'what are we, how did we come to be so, where are we meant to go from here?' Inquiry in depth is injecting a fresh element into the national scene, an element*

of reappraisal. From this, a new and acceptable patriotism, a new sense of national vocation may surely come. The quest for Arthur's Britain cannot be the only factor in such a renewal, but it can be – indeed, it already is – a stimulus.

Glastonbury, though only tenuously linked to Cadbury, was central to Ashe's agenda, and indeed, in some ways, *The Quest* was a restatement of his earlier manifesto:

Glastonbury was, and is, great enough not to need the more dubious legends that have clustered around it. To this day, Arthur's Britain can still be found there, if the Holy Grail cannot ... Enthusiasts have predicted that Glastonbury's future, in some way which cannot yet be foreseen, will be greater than its past. That is the sort of hope which inspires the Chalice Well Trust, the sponsoring body of the Tor excavations. Archaeology, of course, produces the most concrete results. But many who have taken part in Glastonbury's renewal find themselves exploring the mystery by other paths. To act thoughtfully in these surroundings is to ask questions, and to ask rightly is to discover. The quest which this book surveys would not have moved into the high tempo of the 1960s without the impulse given by people whose first Arthurian concern was the resurrection of Avalon.

THE CHALICE WELL GATEWAY

The Chalice Well Trust was set up by Wellesley Tudor Pole, who in 1959 acquired the Chalice Well. This remarkable man, a respectable flour merchant in his working life, was also a visionary writer of some power who knew himself to be in regular connection with forces of the Light from *au-delà* ('beyond'). He was a religious universalist who believed that all true paths led to the same place; he worked with Padre Pio in the Thirties, helped to save the life of the Bahá'í leader Abdu'l-Bahá in the First World War, and in 1940 convinced Winston Churchill to inaugurate a 'Silent Minute' on BBC radio just after Big Ben struck nine each evening. The idea was to draw the nation together for a moment of contemplation, reflection, and/or active prayer during the worst moments of the Second World War, but the Minute was kept up until 1961, making it one of the world's most successful exercises in mass-meditation, although people didn't call it that.

In 1959 TP turned 75, but he was just getting into his stride. Soon after the finding of the Blue Bowl in 1907, TP had been told by a voice from *au-delà* that manuscripts which would throw light on the Bowl's origins and its connection with first-century Christianity were hidden somewhere in Constantinople. Between 1908 and 1953, he made no less than five well-funded attempts to discover these "Jesus scripts" (his term), sometimes with professional archaeologists in tow, but without success. Now fate had presented him with the

Wellesley Tudor
Pole, the old
Merlin (Chalice
Well Trust)

Chalice Well, which, he believed, was "the Gateway" through which the Christian message first reached the West; and he proceeded to apply the same energy he'd given to the Constantinople quests to scouring the holiest earth of Glastonbury for evidence to prove it. The Trust launched an ambitious programme of professional excavation, led by the young Philip Rahtz, a rising star in the archaeological pantheon. He began with the Well itself, but the results were underwhelming, revealing but "slight indications" of Roman and pre-Roman work. Rahtz then moved on to the summit of the Tor itself: "Its proximity to the great spring of Chalice Well suggested that here might be the nucleus of any pagan religious activity in Glastonbury, and this in turn might have acted as a spur to early Christian missionaries."

The dig began in August 1964 in a blaze of publicity, and the following year TP was convinced that they'd dug up a sizeable building "far earlier in date" than the Abbey, but in this he was wrong. Instead, the dig found evidence of something that Rahtz initially interpreted as a Dark Age chieftain's stronghold. He later decided that the hilltop site could indeed have been a religious settlement, but either way it was several centuries too late to support TP's theory. "Archaeologists draw a blank," the headlines declared in August 1966, "but the Chalice Well Trust ... have not given up." Rahtz's third Glastonbury dig, at Beckery (Bride's Mound), which began in 1967, saw the excavation of what he took to be a late Saxon monastery (more recent work suggests that the site was older, with radiocarbon dates from the fifth century which, although not early enough for TP, makes it quite possibly the earliest monastic site in Britain, but that's another story).

ST. MICHAEL AND THE TOR

Proving past legends was only a small part of TP's mission at Chalice Well, however. Preparing for the future was much more important. TP had had surprisingly little to do with Glastonbury during the previous half-century, but he had devoted a lot of his energies to 'rekindling' centres dedicated to the cult of St. Michael. During the Middle Ages, many hilltop sites around Christendom were topped with chapels or churches dedicated to the archangel, who became associated with the suppression of non-Christian forces since pagan temples were often to be found on hilltops. His role as leader of the spiritual forces of light meant that some saw him as having a crucial part to play as harbinger of the Second Coming. To Tudor Pole, "In the 'latter days' of this present age, it is St. Michael and his hosts who are to be the preparers of the way for the Coming of the Christ in glory to rule over the Kingdoms of this world."

The church on Glastonbury Tor had been dedicated to St. Michael; and since the Tor was such a prominent feature, Glastonbury was widely seen as one of the most important 'Michael' sites in the country. It was also a place of conflicting energies. In the Thirties, Dion Fortune, who was both pagan and Christian, thought that the serpent that Michael suppressed represented an ancient wisdom gone to corruption and decadence, yet which was still "a mine of the profoundest knowledge." Michael was "the mighty regent of the element of fire. Who but he should be implored to hold down the serpent of fire-worship, fallen on decadence?" The Tor, she believed, was the "Hill of Vision," even though it was a place where "the

Devil has the best of it." Others were less positive. To 'Chavarinis', the Tor was the "Hill of Evil" – and since she was St. Michael's channel on earth, this was presumably the opinion of the Archangel himself. Chavarinis, more prosaically known as Mrs De Vere Smith, moved to Glastonbury when the Second World War began, and set up the Winds of Truth sanctuary to propagate her archangelic revelations. During the War, Dion Fortune encouraged members of the Fraternity of the Inner Light to visualise a great protective force within the Tor. Chavarinis and her followers fought their own bizarre battle against the forces of darkness, which culminated in the Second Coming of Christ to Glastonbury in June 1941, and his final ascent from Chalice Hill that Michaelmas.

Few others felt that the Second Coming had come and gone so soon, least of all Wellesley Tudor Pole, whose commitment to the cause of Michael was total. Between 1904 and 1966, TP claimed to have helped to rekindle twenty-five centres in Britain and abroad – notably in Iona, and Glastonbury which, he said, "was dead, or anyway in a coma, spiritually speaking" – until the Blue Bowl episode. In 1930, he visited the three sites he felt to be most significant: Iona, Devenish (near Enniskillen, in Ulster), and (in November) Glastonbury; and to him this "conscious relinking of the three points of the triangle of Power" marked the beginnings of "a new Dispensation … the dawn of a Time of Wisdom and Understanding." It was to none of these three points, however, but to Cornwall that he looked for the first glimmerings of the light. In 1928, on St. Michael's Mount near the tip of Cornwall, he had a vision of a "spiritual renaissance" that was gradually coming, via these "psychic centres" – there was "a living psychic strand linking these 'spiritual lungs' of our nation". His vision took him into night sky, from where he looked down on the British Isles and watched "the light radiation from the various centres and the pulsating chains of 'fire' that linked them together." St. Michael's Mount was the touch-paper, and he called upon the people of Cornwall to prepare the way: "Let Cornwall light the Lamp that is to cast its radiance across the whole of Britain and beyond." These words were published in a curious little pamphlet TP edited called *Michael, Prince of Heaven*, published in time for the 1951 Festival of Britain, an event intended to raise the spirits of a nation worn down by war, rationing and a sense of spiralling national decline. No matter that the Welfare State had just been created, and a National Health Service set up that was and still is the envy of the world; to Tudor Pole (and many others), "the deep-seated integrity of the British character seems to be slipping away into a condition of nation-wide futility and frustration." Global political and economic leadership had passed to America and Russia; Britain was in "the Valley of Humiliation." Rekindling the Michael centres, promoting his cult in every way, would pave the way for Christ's return so that "Britain may lead the peoples of the world out of their present darkness into the Light of a New Day."

Setting up the Chalice Well Trust eight years later was an integral part of this vision and the culmination of his life's work, finishing the business begun half a century earlier with the discovery of the Blue Bowl, which in his mind had awoken the spirit of Glastonbury: but for that event, "Avalon and Chalice Well would still lie supine in the shadows, impotent to play their part in the reawakening of Britain and her people to their spiritual destiny." The Chalice Well, he believed, could become a Gateway once again, "through which Christ's message for the New Age can enter and spread across the world. This very holy spot could in fact become once more the sounding board for a revelation of Divine Wisdom, attuned to the desperate needs of today's humanity."

The revival of the Chalice Well certainly triggered renewed interest in the archangelic energies. There was "a concentration of power" around Glastonbury at Michaelmas in 1964, according to June Marsden, an Australian astro-ufologist who was staying in Dion Fortune's old house, Chalice Orchard, on the side of the Tor. A big crowd turned out to witness the newly-formed Order of Bards, Ovates and Druids hold their first function on the Tor, which was "entirely enveloped by soft shiny blue light" according to members of a psychic group called the Universal Link. Their visions and experiences in and around the town that month were published in a booklet in January 1965, which they called *The Michael Power of Glastonbury*. Amongst the Link's more influential followers were Peter and

Most depictions of St Michael show the dragon at the wrong end of the archangelic weapon, but in this curious carved emblem, presented to Iona Abbey by Tudor Pole in 1963, it's the dragon that gives the sword its power

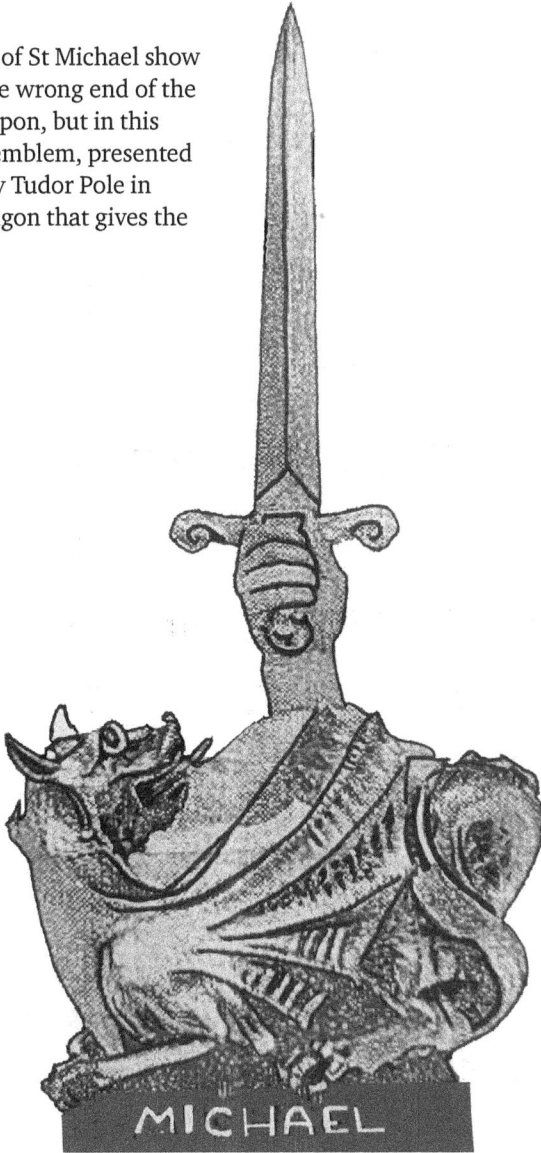

Eileen Caddy, founders of the Findhorn Community in Scotland. Eileen had had the vision that set them on the path to Findhorn during a meditation at the Winds of Truth sanctuary years before – and at Michaelmas in

1965, she had another one, this time of the Archangel Michael: "He had a foot in Glastonbury and a foot in Findhorn and a sword pointing to Iona, as if uniting the three." That summer, Peter Caddy had met Tudor Pole and, "emphatically stating that he was the guardian of Glastonbury," urged him to prepare the town for the thousands of young people who would soon be drawn to the place. Plans were afoot to acquire the lease on the Tor House School next door for a healing and spiritual centre and, that November, a Glastonbury Foundation was set up, with Caddy as roving ambassador, fundraiser and putative warden. But TP was unenthusiastic. A spiritual healing centre "would attract cranks mostly, and create hostile attitudes locally," he explained to a friend, and he found a patron to buy the school buildings for the Chalice Well Trust instead. The Foundation soon foundered, Caddy put his energies into Findhorn, and TP continued to prepare the Well for the Second Coming, but more of that in a bit.

UNIDENTIFIED FLYING ZODIAC

The dig at Cadbury/Camelot attracted a lot of arcane interest, and since Geoffrey Ashe himself never missed an opportunity of linking Glastonbury and Cadbury, it is hardly surprising that others did so too. Amongst those exploring the mystery was Jess Foster, inspired by Ashe to found the Pendragon Society in 1959, which was dedicated to Arthurian studies and research into the 'Matter of Britain'. The group held a Pendragon Party in 1966 to raise funds for the Cadbury dig, at which Foster talked to Jimmy Goddard, one of the leading lights of the Ley Hunters' Club, about the many straight tracks she believed criss-crossed the area around Cadbury, and asked if their members could help discover the tranche of "King Arthur's causeway" that was said to have linked the hillfort to Glastonbury.

It was an interesting overlap. The Ley Hunters' Club had been set up by three young UFO watchers, inspired by the work of Tony Wedd who believed that flying saucers followed ley routes. Leys were first perceived by Alfred Watkins in the early 1920s as tracks of possibly massive antiquity that crossed the country in straight lines (his book, *The Old Straight Track*, caused quite a furore when it was published in 1925: much more on this in the "Straight Track to Beyond" section of my most excellent *Creating Prehistory*). Wedd's work suggested a connection between the ancient terrestrial landscape and the activities of the visitors from outer space whose existence so tantalised the post-war subconscious. In the rational 1950s, ufology filled something of the gap that romance left. However, the evidence for the physical existence of UFOs was so contradictory that Carl Jung, in his 1959 book, *Flying Saucers: A Modern Myth of Things Seen in the Skies*, concluded that the UFO phenomenon was essentially psychic in nature, one of those "manifestations of psychic changes which always appear at the end of one Platonic month and at the beginning of another

... which bring about, or accompany, long-lasting transformations of the collective psyche" – in other words, the dawning of the Age of Aquarius.

According to Brinsley le Poer Trench, a former editor of the *Flying Saucer Review*, the key to understanding the transition between the Ages lay in the Glastonbury Zodiac, which had been created by the Atlanteans and the Sky People as a memorial that would survive the Deluge: "It is to Glastonbury and to the Temple of the Stars that we must look for information regarding our immediate future." "We" being the British in particular. "When the true significance and understanding of the Somerset Zodiac is really grasped, the British people will realise that they have on their soil a monument from the past, which will help them to understand not only the present but also the future. *A legacy from their Atlantean forebears which is infinitely greater than either Stonehenge or the Great Pyramid in Egypt.*" Britain may have lost an empire, but the world was turning our way all the same. The Zodiac was "the most sacred spot on earth."

As above, so below. Maltwood's *The Temple of the Stars* was long out of print, but in 1964 a cheap reprint appeared. According to the dust-jacket, these "gigantic earth monuments of a primitive people ... appear to be a land chart of the sky" – a useful aid for alien navigation perhaps. June Marsden, Australia's first newspaper astrologer, chartered a plane in May of 1964 to check out the Zodiac, and declared that

Libra – the Dove, painting by Osmund Caine (1966)

she'd found 19 signs instead of the usual 12. Marsden was a prominent ufologist, who had once entertained George Adamski, the most famous contactee of them all, and indeed fell out with him over her attempt to link astrology and ufology ("I explained to her that no connection existed between the two," he lamented, "but she refused to accept the logical facts"). It is not clear from her account how the Glastonbury Zodiac served the sky-people, but she agreed with Trench that it was "the number one wonder of the world."

Mary Caine was scarcely less constrained when she declared the Zodiac to be "the greatest discovery that Britain has ever known." She first came across the Zodiac in 1961, and immediately wrote in great enthusiasm to Katherine Maltwood herself, only to be informed by her husband John that his wife has just died. She then embarked on an exuberant but increasingly tactless correspondence with the widower, in which hopes for a potential TV series were at first welcomed and then rebuffed once she suggested that she might be in some way his late wife's spiritual heir. Undaunted, she turned to her artist husband Osmund for help. Like June Marsden, they hired a plane to survey the Zodiac from above. They made a short film, *The Glastonbury Giants*, which failed to tempt the movie moguls but earned the couple a good-humoured if sceptical feature article by Geoffrey Moorhouse in *The Guardian* when it was launched in January, 1966. It also helped to garner publicity for Osmund's exhibition of rather fine paintings, based on Zodiac features, which went on display in London in September 1966.

That Christmas, on the eve of the *annus mirabilis* that was 1967, the Zodiac idea was picked up and transmitted to a new generation by Brendan Lehane in an article which appeared, of all places, in the festive edition of *The Telegraph Sunday Magazine*. Lehane's piece, called 'Did Christ Come to Britain?', brought the Jesus visit and the Zodiac into the same framework. Where Moorhouse had been sardonic, Lehane was enthusiastic. Maltwood's book, he declared,

> *is ingenious and exciting … The zodiac-earthwork theory may or may not be true … But there are still many who claim that the colossal features were planned and carved in soil some 5,000 years ago, master-minded by – there can be no more surprises – the original Merlin … So, while Christ and Joseph fade, the antique Aura of Glastonbury grows. Yet in growing it makes the Christian legend more plausible … The onus of proof is on the cynics. And there can never be proof, for want of documents. In these conditions, maybe the best recourse is to visionaries.*

One was at hand.

TRANSFORMATION

Enter John Michell, the 'cosmological switchman' who sent a generation off the straight and narrow and onto the old straight track that led to much more interesting places. Flying saucers, the Zodiac and the force of St. Michael all came together in the visionary architect of hippy Glastonbury. He is such an important figure that his work needs looking at in detail.

Michell was of the same ilk as the Chelsea set, though maybe not as wealthy. He'd sunk his inheritance in property around some of the less fashionable parts of London, including a house near Victoria Station which he shared for a while with Andrew Kerr, later of Glastonbury Fair fame, where he ran an after-hours club ostensibly designed to raise funds for canal restoration (that house backed onto my parents' flat, not they were aware of each others' existence: did my infant howlings disturb their after-hours drinking, or did their rowdiness keep me awake? Did I imbue some cosmic vibes from over the fence?). His investments came unstuck when a partner turned rogue and absconded to South Africa, costing him much of his lucre, but he retained at least one very run-down house in Notting Hill, where he lived on and off for most of his life. It was a much grittier and more grounded place than Chelsea – dynamic and exciting, and home to a whole tribe of scene-setters and makers, amongst them Michell's friend Alex Trocchi, Situationist publisher and acid pioneer. Trocchi was a crucial figure in the LSD subculture of those early-Sixties years when it was still legal – "His flat became a focus for those wanting to buy, use or discuss the amazing new substance," says Andy Roberts – and it seems likely that he introduced it to Michell since, on his own reckoning (he was born in 1933), he made the discovery as early as 1963:

> *Most of my contemporaries had made it, and were*
> *successful by that time, so they don't know what it's*

like for a failure aged 30 to become an acid freak. It was marvellous. A head stuffed full of liberal, academic nonsense was spun around, and new patterns of thought appeared, far more natural and interesting than any which had been offered by the education process.

He once called LSD's discoverer, Albert Hofmann, a "Promethean hero." Like Prometheus, who stole fire back from the gods, Hofmann had taken vision back from the priests.

In the summer of 1964, according to his friend Neil Oram, Michell was planning on going to Mongolia, perhaps to escape from his business woes. Oram suggested that he should read up on UFO literature instead, and "told him my theory that I thought Stonehenge and such places were TRANSFORMING STATIONS." According to Oram, Michell was immediately impressed, started tripping in ancient places at night, and was duly TRANSFORMED. He began to research the phenomenon more fully and, at the end of 1965, he heard a talk by Jimmy Goddard at Kensington Library linking leys and UFOs: a significant moment, though it took him a while to realise it himself.

John Michell was a trickster who all his days delighted in discomfiting orthodoxy of any kind, so he was in his element in the rebellious 1960s. He had been profoundly influenced by Carl Jung's interpretation of the UFO phenomenon, and the challenges the concept posed to the smugness of contemporary Western thinking. The first known exposition of his ideas came in a lecture delivered in 1966 (which, incredibly enough, is online) to an unknown but UFO-friendly audience. The title is bracing ("Alien Infiltration"), but the hour-long lecture is controversial in more subtle ways. His starting-point is Jung's contention that the UFO phenomenon was a psychic reaction to the dawning of the New Age. He looks at some length at historical accounts of possible abductees or visiting aliens, but the nub of his case is the claim that dragon-lore equated with memories of flying saucers.

Brinsley Le Poer Trench's aforementioned book had told the ufology world how the eighteenth-century antiquary William Stukeley had decided that ancient sites such as Avebury were 'dracontia' – places where serpent-wisdom was enshrined in monuments and earthworks. John Michell saw such places as evidence of ancient sacrificial cargo-cults aimed at placating or invoking the help of 'dragons' – flying saucers from other worlds. He cites Silbury and Croagh Patrick and the Lambton Worm Hill and Callanish and the White Horse and Stonehenge, but there's nary a mention of Glastonbury (nor, indeed, leys). It wasn't until that summer, according to the useful introduction Michell penned many years later for *The Sun and the Serpent*, that he visited the place for the first time. He hitchhiked down from London, via Avebury, with Beat poet and fellow acid-head Harry Fainlight, and it is clear that Harry's preoccupations shaped the trip. How else to explain why the future author of *The Flying Saucer Vision,* which he was then busily researching, failed to visit Warminster when they headed west? That small Wiltshire town had become the ufologists' Mecca in 1965; on August Bank Holiday alone, over 8,000 visitors came to scan its skies. It was on the road from Avebury to Glastonbury, yet they didn't go near the place. So what was Harry Fainlight looking for?

BLAKE, THE BEATS AND THE BIRTH OF THE NEW AGE

According to Jonathon Green, some say the Sixties started in 1965, "when every beatnik aspiration seemed to climax, listening to poetry at the Albert Hall;" others, equally, saw that event as the end of them. A pedant might point out that 1965, being bang-smack in the middle of the decade, can hardly have marked either the start or the end of it, but at any rate it's clear enough that the International Poetry Incarnation which happened that June was a pretty major turning-point.

The organisers were much under the spell of Allen Ginsberg, greatest of the Beat poets and himself hugely inspired by William Blake. "Rouze up, O Young Men of the New Age! Set your foreheads against the ignorant hirelings!", Blake had declared. Ginsberg believed that now was the time. As his friend Tom Clark said,

PREFACE.

The Stolen and Perverted Writings of Homer &
Ovid: of Plato & Cicero. which all Men ought to
contemn: are set up, by artifice against the Sublime
of the Bible. but when the New Age is at leisure
to Pronounce; all will be set right & those Grand
Works of the more ancient & consciously & profes-
sedly Inspired Men. will hold their proper rank &
the Daughters of Memory shall become the Daughters of Inspiration. Shakspeare & Milton were
both curbd by the general malady & infection from
the silly Greek & Latin slaves of the Sword.—
Rouze up O Young Men of the New Age! set your
foreheads against the ignorant Hirelings! For
we have Hirelings in the Camp, the Court & the Uni
versity: who would if they could, for ever depress Mental
& prolong Corporeal War. Painters! on you I call!
Sculptors! Architects! Suffer not the fashionable Fools
to depress your powers by the prices they pretend to
give for contemptible works or the expensive advertizing
boasts that they make of such works; believe
Christ & his Apostles that there is a Class of Men
whose whole delight is in Destroying. We do not
want either Greek or Roman Models if we are but
just & true to our own Imaginations. those Worlds
of Eternity in which we shall live for ever; in
Jesus our Lord.

And did those feet in ancient time.
Walk upon Englands mountains green:
And was the holy Lamb of God.
On Englands pleasant pastures seen!

And did the Countenance Divine.
Shine forth upon our clouded hills?
And was Jerusalem builded here.
Among these dark Satanic Mills?

Bring me my Bow of burning gold:
Bring me my Arrows of desire:
Bring me my Spear: O clouds unfold:
Bring me my Chariot of fire!

I will not cease from Mental Fight.
Nor shall my Sword sleep in my hand:
Till we have built Jerusalem.
In Englands green & pleasant Land

Would to God that all the Lords people
were Prophets   Numbers XI.ch 29.v

William Blake, "Preface" to *Milton: A Poem in Two Books* 1804–1810

"Ginsberg's idea of a Jerusalemic Britain occurring now in the day of long hair and new music meant equally the fulfilment of Blake's predictions of Albion." The Incarnation began with an Invocation, devised by ten of the organisers including Ginsberg and Fainlight (and also Alex Trocchi and John Esam, of whom more anon – it was a small world), prefaced by six lines from *Jerusalem* (the prophetic book, not the song) that were printed on the programme as a manifesto:

> *"England! Awake! awake! awake!*
> *Jerusalem thy sister calls!*
> ..
> *And now the time returns again:*
> *Our souls exult, and London's towers*
> *Receive the Lamb of God to dwell*
> *in England's green and pleasant bowers."*

Harry Fainlight had been one of the poets to read, but his poem, *Spider*, about a bad LSD trip, did not go down well, and Ginsberg was indignant on Fainlight's behalf. It was possibly this event that prompted Ginsberg's personal pilgrimage to Glastonbury, where he sought to rouse something lacking in Albion's bardic tradition: according to Tom Clark, "he stood in the chilly drizzle over what was said to be the grave of King Arthur and chanted an extended, improvised rabbinical-druidic hymn. It evoked the strength and innocence of Blake's Albion and ended on what seemed to me, at the time, a strange remark, perhaps a challenge hurled from king to king: 'British poets are cowardly!'"

Ginsberg was close to Fainlight, and his visit probably inspired Harry's the following year. Both were Jewish, and both, according to John Michell, were stirred by Blake's address to the Jews, in which he had told them not only that their traditions came from the Druids, but also that the heavenly Jerusalem would appear in England. This made the country the natural homeland for the Jews, a concept that strongly influenced Fainlight. And if you're in England and looking for Jerusalem, then Glastonbury was the obvious place to go. Blake's rousing Preface to his prophetic book *Milton*, known now to the world as 'Jerusalem', suggested that Christ himself had visited England, and although it is highly unlikely that Blake had any specific English Mountains Green in mind for Those Feet to walk on, least of all Glastonbury, Lionel Smithett Lewis, the 1920s vicar of Glastonbury, decided that Christ had indeed visited his parish, and adopted 'Jerusalem' as "the Glastonbury hymn." Geoffrey Ashe cemented the presumed connection between Blake and Glastonbury for the new generation by assuming unquestioningly that Blake did have Glastonbury in mind: "Blake's instinct was sound. Glastonbury is England's only real national shrine, and a Glastonbury legend, however unlikely, is one of the few adequate themes for a national hymn."

So, it seems that John Michell's first trip to Glastonbury was in pursuit of someone else's agenda,

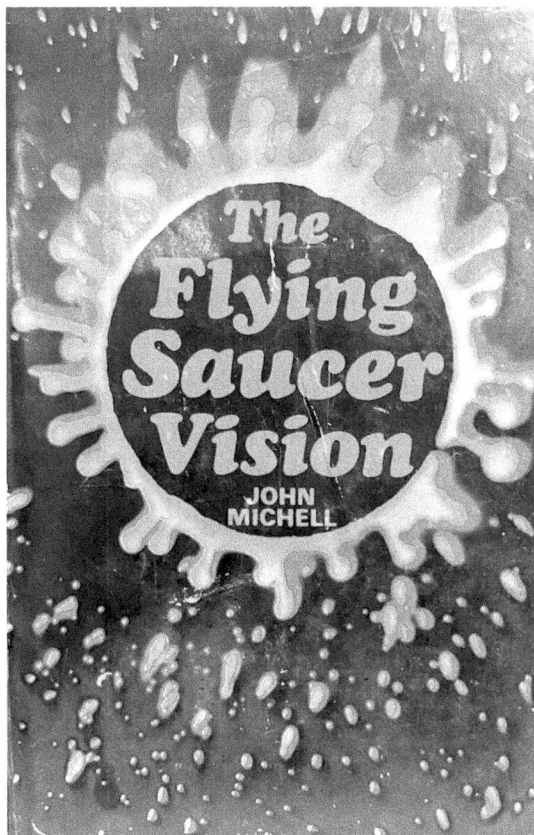

and at that point Harry's concerns failed to pique his curiosity overmuch, since the book he was then researching, *The Flying Saucer Vision*, makes no mention of either Blake or Albion. The book covers the same ground as the "Alien Infiltration" lecture, less luridly and in a bit more detail. We learn that folkloric references to dragons and flying saucers were "invariably interchangeable" – dragon hills and similar landmarks were connected by ley lines which, since they were only visible from the air, "substantiates the legend that these places were the centre of a sky-god cult, raised platforms where contact with the flying gods was made and sacrifices offered". St. Michael was a Christianised "revered being" from a distant star, and the many hilltop St. Michael sites "were once associated with the memory of a being from the sky and of the dragon disc." The most famous of these was Glastonbury: "Here is Avalon, the paradise of Arthurian romance. From Glastonbury Tor, men left earth to join the gods," willingly or otherwise; he saw Henry VIII's grisly execution of Abbot Whiting and his two monks on the Tor-top as a perversion of "the old practice of offering men to the gods from the sky." As to the Zodiac, "whether or not some great sculpted message to the sky gods does lie below Glastonbury Tor, as Miss Maltwood describes, there is no doubt that the whole area was particularly sacred to the early flying saucer cult." The meaning of the message, he suggests, must have been known only to initiates, but it was information that might perhaps be recoverable. The "rediscovery" of the Zodiac, he claimed, "has been a notable step in the modern revival of astrology," a revival which, he elsewhere suggests, might be seen as evidence "of some kind of external influence in our affairs, or even the influence itself at work to prepare us for the changes we must now expect."

But that's about it for Glastonbury. Three pages out of 170, a fraction of the space he devoted to other topics, and the emphasis was firmly on communication with the sky gods. Next year, everything changed.

CHAPTER TWO

1967

BEAUTIFUL INSIDE

T*he Flying Saucer Vision* was a pioneering work, recasting the whole UFO phenomenon as a change of consciousness whose effects were visibly manifesting all around us: as Paul Screeton neatly puts it, Michell "transferred the concept of spaceships from outer to inner space." The Sixties revolution was evidence of extraterrestrial forces at work, a kind of extrinsic download, actually happening now; the lights in the sky were portents of the Age of Aquarius, in much the same way as the Star of Bethlehem had portended the Age of Pisces. "There are elements of vegetarianism, Eastern philosophy, a messianic cult and the folklore of technology all fused together by the catalyst of flying saucers. It may be said that this was the first popular attempt to develop a way of thought for the New Age," he wrote. "A recent development in which some see an approaching revolution in our attitudes of thought is the increasingly wide interest in the use of drugs. Occurring at a time when no further progress seems possible within the present system, their appearance as 'deus ex machina' to expand the limits of experience is remarkably opportune. It is hardly likely that their development and use at this very time can be a matter of pure chance." This phrase, which as Andy Roberts says "summed up the hopes and aspirations surrounding the early use of psychedelics," explains why John Michell himself later claimed the book to be "a genuine artefact of 1967," but it was not. It was a genuine artefact of 1966. It was sent to the publisher in January 1967, and a lot had changed by the time the book came out in November.

Something major happened late that summer of 1967 to ground the Glastonbury vision. While the eight-year-old me was taking his place in Miss Peers' class and learning with the rest to sing 'All Things Bright and Beautiful', a bunch of beautiful people from the King's Road abandoned their boutiques, left the city and went horse-drawn across the English countryside to Glastonbury, and John Michell went with them.

John was at the heart of Bohemia. In 1966, the London Free School set up in the basement of his house in Notting Hill, with high ambitions that mostly came to naught (the enormous exception being the Notting Hill Fair and Pageant, the first of the Notting Hill Carnivals: curious, that Michell should be implicated in the origins of Britain's two largest music events). As John himself said, it "was not so much a school as a dank cellar, furnished with a fireplace and a teapot," but it did bring together a lot of movers and shakers: "In the fetid atmosphere of the Free School the Sixties culture flourished and went on to infect Chelsea." That summer, he chartered two large canal boats to bring the Free School and Chelsea communities together "for a fortnights' adventuring among the mysteries of the English landscape." Things didn't go according to plan, but Jane Rainey was one of those who, in later years, Michell remembered as having helped to save the day. Born Jane Ormsby-Gore, she and her sisters were already celebrities, at the heart of Sixties fashion culture. Her husband Michael Rainey, according to Nik Cohn, street fashion historian, was "the most original designer that English menswear has produced." His shop, Hung On You, "was simultaneously the last fling of dandyism and the first intimation of Hippie, of strangenesses to come"; his customers included the Rolling Stones, the Beatles and the Kinks.

To people like the Raineys, fashion meant a lot more than just the look of things. They were dreamers and visionaries, Michael Rainey particularly so: "His idealistic foresights of a new world, shortly to be revealed, of perfect beauty and harmony, stunned even his wide-minded contemporaries," in Michell's words. In the summer of '67, his wares were much modelled by moody young men from his friend Sir Mark Palmer's pioneering English Boy agency. Palmer, as Cohn pithily puts it, "had served three years in the hulks, as pageboy to H.M. the Queen" and had been such a sartorial stickler that he once spent forty minutes on the phone discussing what tie to wear. Now, according to Maureen Cleave, interviewer of many Sixties icons, he underwent a heart-and-soul metamorphosis "so complete as to transcend mere affectation." The English Boy agency lasted little more than six months: it was a manifestation, a happening, part of a much bigger scene in which folk like Palmer and the Raineys saw themselves as pathfinders: prototypes, as the name implied, for a new sort of England. "'The English Boys are not just models but model *people*, models for other people to model themselves on,'" Palmer told Cleave. "'By our appearance we are indicating our way of life, the way we think, the way we feel. This is our way of getting under the public skin, turning them on to what we believe and like. Our appearance is indicative of our inner scene." He borrows words. "It's an outward manifestation of an inner grace. I think appearances are so important. The English Boys must look beautiful, they must look as though they're beautiful *inside*. … He is obsessed with looks, with health, magic and yoga. His conversation is about mind-expansion, the destruction of barriers in the mind, merging his mind with the mind of the Infinite; about beauty, purity, honesty, states of love, codes of sensitivity.'" Also, she could have added, food. Palmer, like Michell and the others, were pioneers on the healthy-eating trail, vegetarians, into macrobiotics. Committed to the lifestyle.

JOURNEY TO THE CENTRE OF THE WORLD

"Mark is something of a fashion oracle," declared Nadeane Walker, fashion editor for Associated Press, in a much-syndicated article that appeared in early September. According to her, he was planning to take the English Boy to New York, but by the time the interview came out, Palmer had moved on, quite literally. As the Summer of Love drew to a close, *ennui* set in amongst the *haut hipoisie*. Its leading lights began to feel more and more jaded with the scene which they themselves had helped to create. Some of them, like Palmer, cut free completely. In the flippantly evocative words of Marianne Faithfull

> *Sir Mark Palmer – but let's just call him "Mark" for fuck's sake! – spent the late sixties on a quest for the Holy Grail in the caravan with loads of exquisitely dressed people. "Why don't we travel across the land like gypsies and be free?" Mark asked, and since nobody could see any reasonable (or unreasonable) objection (they were all as stoned as he), they bought a barrel-top gypsy wagon and a brown and white horse they dubbed Rizla, and off they went in search of the ineffable, unfindable, once-and-future whatnot. A whimsical itinerary: Camelot, Glastonbury Tor, Tintagel (where Arthur, it's said, was conceived), Boscastle (where Merlin lived), Launceston (supposedly Sir Lancelot's town – although better known for its steam railway – and flying saucers, of course. How they came into a quest for the Holy Grail was ... oh, never mind ... It took them four years to get to Wales, for heaven's sake – so a lot of detours to investigate mounds and*

*tors, and ley lines and Arthurian antiquariana.
They were living in this quasi-medieval bubble that
had nothing to do with the straight world – all the
magical, mystical, lysergic lore of the sixties taken to
extreme extremes.*

By the time the great trek ended, in 1971, practically
the whole of Chelsea had joined them for a while; as
Felix Attagong says, the roll-call reads like "a who-
is-who of Swingin' London." "It was a motley crew,"
recalls Faithfull. "Some of them just came and went …
Then there were real hard-cores who signed on for
the entire quest … All sorts of people were looking
for the Holy Grail, but it was Mark's mission." It was
one he took very seriously, too seriously for Marianne
Faithfull. The food was macrobiotic, the acid was
sacramental, and random hedonism was seriously
frowned upon. There was a "very strict hippie rule book
about food and drugs – except for LSD … Mark was
very doctrinaire about the lysergic pieties – the way
acid heads sometimes get, funny thing, that … Which
is why I would never go on these caravans. Never did.
I loved the thought if it, you know: loved the idea that
there were loads of my friends going round England all
the time in search of the Holy Grail."

Palmer set out with two friends, Martin Wilkinson
and Maldwyn Thomas, English Boy models, by catching
the train to Didcot. They kipped out on the Berkshire
Downs, and bought a dung-cart from a dealer. "That
was the start – and we set off," recalled Maldwyn. They

headed west, into the heart of England, much as H.V. Morton had done forty years earlier when he set off to write *In Search of England*, his best-selling quest for the soul of the land, but it is very telling that they went horse-drawn along the Ridgeway and not, as Morton had done, in a snazzy motor out along the Bath Road. Theirs was a retrospective trip, and the pace of the journey was important. Travelling on the green roads at four miles per hour, soaking up the countryside, was the rhythm of this most psychidyllic journey. The English Boys were soon joined by Jane and Michael Rainey with their baby son Saffron, and also by John Michell, the team Merlin, who understood their mission perfectly:

> *The purpose of their travels was not just to enjoy themselves but to enact and foster throughout England the spirit of the New Age. Everyone who joined them, however hopeless, was accepted as a co-religionist. They took to the road in the same colourful finery as they wore in Chelsea. Silk scarves trailed in the mud, and rain-bedraggled their wisps and velvets, but these outfits were not meant to be practical in the grey sense of the word – they were the sacerdotal garments of New Age missionaries.*

When Palmer was done for dope possession in September of 1968, he went to court wearing a gold silk waistcoat, leaf-patterned shirt and yellow velvet trousers, and there were chrysanthemums on his cart:

details lovingly captured by the journalists and relayed to a world now hungry for colour.

ST. MICHAEL AND THE DRAGON LINE

Like H.V. Morton, the travellers headed straight for Glastonbury. "I thought that if a man were looking for the roots of England, this is the place to which he would come," wrote Morton in 1927. The Flower Children of '67 were looking for something deeper still, and at Glastonbury they found it. Michael Rainey's epiphany was Arthurian: "I got this vision of the Arthurian legend, and I thought, 'Wow, this is for real,' and I embarked on this Arthurian search and started chasing it around the country" (to the considerable detriment of Hung On You, it must be said; he finally sold the business in early '69 to go horse-drawn with his family and team up properly with Mark Palmer for a few months before heading off to the Mediterranean in search of new adventures). The appeal of Arthuriana to the Chelsea romantics is not surprising, particularly since the Cadbury-Camelot dig had just begun that summer in a blaze of publicity, but these first New Age travellers, these "New Age grail questers," as John Michell called them, were on the track of something far more elusive and mystical than a Dark Age chieftain and his lair. They were "searching for UFOs, ley lines and other totems of the Age of Aquarius."

Something was certainly stirring in Glastonbury that summer. At the solstice, on the Tor, the Brotherhood of the Essenes proclaimed that Glastonbury was the "appointed spot" for the Second Advent which could happen "very very soon." And in August, Tudor Pole gave his Annual Message to Companions and friends of Chalice Well, in which he told them that the Upper Room in Little St. Michael's was about to be furnished with a Table and thirteen stools, laid out as for the Last Supper, and would "in due course" acquire a second table laid as for "Breakfast," "facing the gardens and the orchards, with Michael's Tor on the horizon; and it is across this scene that the rising sun will cast its radiance."

The passing of the Age of Pisces and the coming of Aquarius were thus to be celebrated in the same room. This concept was catnip to any New Age totem-seeker, and although there's no proof that the travellers had heard of TP's Annual Message, copies were on sale at the Chalice Well for half-a-crown, so they might well have done. They certainly made a thing of visiting the Well, initially to Tudor Pole's consternation. These were not the sort of New Age missionaries he'd been hoping for. "Last Sunday [i.e. September 17th], a group of 'flower' folk invaded C.W. gardens, led by Lord Harlech's errant daughter [Jane Rainey] (with, I believe, her year old baby). They did no harm but the press published the story with pictures of Chalice Well; and we are trying to make it clear that the C.W.T. dissociates itself from cults of all kinds." Some might say that that was a bit rich, coming from him, but not

Michael, Jane and Saffron Rainey invade the Chalice Well garden
(Brian Walker)

even visionaries always see clearly. I like that word
"errant". He meant 'off the rails', but errantry is what
questing is all about. "Life is an adventure," as Jane
told the journalists.

The shots the paparazzi got featured the Flower
Children appropriately admiring flowers in the Chalice
Well Garden, and Michael hit the rhetorical high notes
a couple of days later:

Flower People seek 'The Truth' in Glastonbury

rang out the headline in the town's newspaper, the
Central Somerset Gazette, on September 22nd.

Town is 'centre of the world'.

The Beatles' psychedelic coach could be among a huge 'pilgrimage' of 'flower people' to Glastonbury within the coming weeks.

The past weekend has seen the early pilgrims who have been to Glastonbury in search of 'the truth' and some of them believe great things are about to happen in Glastonbury ... Michael Rainey "told a 'Gazette' reporter that as soon as they arrived in Glastonbury they felt a certain atmosphere.

He and Jane agreed that they had learned much from their visit. "Glastonbury is the centre of the world," said Michael, "from it everything emanates."

The psychedelic coach never materialised and the pilgrimage that year was far from huge, but these questors were well-known, highly visible, young and confident, and clearly in the vanguard of a major social movement. Their friend Camilla Drummond told another journalist that Glastonbury was "the spiritual capital" of Britain: "Friends had been carrying out researches at Glastonbury on such things as the Glastonbury Zodiac, she said. The Zodiac was proving more apparent every day as well as the 'almost factual burial of Christ here and all the implications that arise from that.'" Make of that what you will; she was younger than the others (only 21), being hassled for comment by a journalist who wanted a story outside a court that had just fined her rather steeply for drugs possession. I'd have been a lot more incoherent myself in those circumstances. What I detect is a growing conviction, a mounting sense of excitement. The travellers spent many hours on the Tor-top meditating, they told journalists, for Glastonbury, they believe, will be the centre of the 'spiritual renaissance'. This truly was the moment at which the New Age came alive at Glastonbury.

THE DRAGON AWAKES

Michael Rainey's comments seem to echo William Blake's famous phrase, "All things begin and end in Albion's ancient Druid rocky shore," which John Michell would soon make much of, so maybe they'd been reading Blake on their gentle magical journey through the English countryside at the tail-end of a summer like no other. It's interesting though that they did not get their information from anything that Michell had yet written. His consciousness was expanding just as theirs was. The travellers were engaged in researching 'secrets of the landscape,' reporters were told. "One of the group," almost certainly John Michell himself, told them of alignments between the Tor, Silbury Hill, Burrow Mump and St. Michael's Mount, far away in Cornwall. These secrets needed unravelling; then the time will be right for "the landing of people from other worlds, the second coming of Christ, and the manifestation of the new spirit."

The first secret was revealed in an article that John sent to his friend John Esam, who published it several months later in his quarterly glossy magazine *The Image*. "Lung Mei and the Dragon Paths of England" is a manifesto for the dream of hippy Glastonbury but in later life it seems Michell had forgotten even writing it: it would probably not be known at all but for Paul Screeton, who came across a copy at a friend's house. He (John) had mentioned Lung Mei in *The Flying Saucer Vision*, citing as his source Luther Newton Hayes' 1922 book, *The Chinese Dragon*. According to Hayes, Lung Mei were "a network of invisible paths of the dragon" across the earth's surface, paths of propitious energy. Hayes' paths were not necessarily straight at all but they were straightened up smartly by Michell to equate them with ley lines. A footnote in John's book states tantalisingly that "Lung Mei, straight lines linking the places associated with the dragon, have recently been traced in Britain," but at that stage they were peripheral to his case since Michell was still looking more skyward than earthward, determined to interpret his dragon lines in terms of routes for extra-terrestrial communication.

The *Image* article begins by joining the dots on a series of dragon-lore sites and identifying two north-south lines, one running from Roxburghshire to Kent, the other from Northumberland to Dorset, and develops into a discussion about the ambivalent qualities of the dragon, which represents both good and evil, yin and yang: "Perhaps in time it will come to represent a third state, the level of super-consciousness of the existence of which we are just becoming aware." Then comes

John Michell in September 1967, the moment of revelation (The John Michell Archive)

the exciting bit: a highly-charged, breathless two-page postscript, headed "The Third Lung Mei," which is printed in italics and dated "Glastonbury, September 21st 1967."

"Signs of an imminent revelation of literally inconceivable scope are now so abundant and clear that only the wilfully blind can be unaware of the change in the psychic atmosphere that 1967 has brought," Michell hyperbolised. The discovery of the third dragon path was a manifestation of this, and his starting point was a copy of Tudor Pole's 1951 pamphlet *Michael, Prince of Heaven*, which he'd picked up at the Chalice Well bookstall when he came with Harry Fainlight the previous year. Quoting an otherwise-unknown piece of folklore, TP had claimed that

In the villages of West Somerset there still exists a tradition which says that: 'the day will come when JESUS THE CHRIST will come striding up the lanes from Cornwall on His way to Avalon,' and the country folk of these parts are warned to be watchful and on the alert, so that He does not pass that way without being recognised and entertained.

He asked pilgrims to make these shrines "worthy stepping-stones for the footsteps of the great Master whom St. Michael serves … It is in such ways that the road will be made straight for One who will surely come if there are sufficient of those who have made themselves worthy of His coming."

In the *Image* article, Michell paraphrases TP's words and conflates them with the story of Arthur's return. Readers were urged to rediscover the principles of geomancy, astrology and alchemy, necessary if old prophecies were to be fulfilled. "Two things we are told: King Arthur is not dead but only sleeping: in Somerset they wait for His second coming along the path from St. Michael's Mount to Glastonbury Tor: we are told to make straight his path." What path could be straighter than the Old Straight Track? Twelve miles west of Glastonbury on the Taunton road, John camped up with Mark Palmer at Burrow Mump, a small but striking hill on the Somerset Levels which, like the Tor, has a church tower on top dedicated to St Michael. He was struck by the "spiritual link" between the two hills, which were both similarly oriented.

Back in Glastonbury to check his evidence, he found an alignment of significant places that ran across the country from St. Michael's Mount to the East Anglian coast. It was the ultimate ley line.

Glastonbury now became the centre of absolutely everything. "At Glastonbury the veil of the Enchantment of Britain lies thinnest. There all things begin and end." Reality had shifted since he'd written *The Flying Saucer Vision*. "There is no surviving dragon story at Glastonbury Tor," he wrote in the book. But in September 1967, we are told that Glastonbury "was the centre of the dragon cult, the system of astronomical study on which the whole glorious tradition of the Druids and their native predecessors was founded." At the mid-point of the third Lung Mei, "St. Michael's tower on Glastonbury Tor overlooks the centre of resistance today, the stubborn town where the new light must blaze before the mysterious giant goddess is awakened. If the light can be kindled there, it will shine as from a lighthouse across the land."

TWO MERLINS

"Lighthouse" was a curious word to use, since Tudor Pole had envisaged a similar role for the Chalice Well. "The beams from the Lighthouse which is within our power to build may well be destined to radiate illumination to the far corners of the Earth," he wrote in *The Silent Road*, published by the Chalice Well Trust in 1960 and on sale at the Chalice Well bookshop alongside *Michael, Prince of Heaven*. Could it be that John Michell picked up a copy of that book too?

It's worth pointing out that John Michell was not the first person to perceive a straight line of energy between the Tor and St. Michael's Mount. Dion Fortune got there over thirty years earlier in her novel *The Goat-Foot God*, when she claimed that these two points, together with Mont-Saint-Michel in Brittany, "make a perfect triangle." The ancient power centres of Britain were linked by "lines of force" which, the story claimed, were still in use by pagans, though the Christians had long since exorcised the power centres themselves by erecting Michael chapels on key hilltops. But the idea probably came from Tudor Pole's vision of the "living psychic strand" that linked the Michael centres; both Dion Fortune and her mother, Sarah Jane Firth, were in contact with him, and her mother was actively involved in his mission to rekindle the Michael sites. Michell was probably unaware of Fortune's novel in 1967, since his interest in Glastonbury had only just been galvanised, but the resonances between his vision and that of Tudor Pole are interesting, and in some ways unexpected. Both of them were dubbed "Merlin" from time to time. They probably wouldn't have recognised each other as such, but in the long run their spellbinding effect on Glastonbury is both comparable and undeniable.

ALBINA

The giant goddess is even more intriguing. In John's words, "It is as if some giantess lies asleep across England, her cyclopean Eye in Suffolk where the alignment of mound, church and abbey point the line, her ankles under the sign of Aquarius at St. Michael's Mount, her Piscean feet on the Sennen peninsular," her body divided by the third Lung Mei.

Within a few weeks of his vision, Michell, who was also a talented artist, got to depict her in large format, elongated like a Giacometti figure, or else a monstrous Barbie, on a wall the size of a restaurant. The Abbey Cafe in Glastonbury's Benedict Street was owned by Gino and Nancy Schiraldi, who had befriended Michell and Harry Fainlight on their first visit and given them a place to stay. Much impressed by John's ideas, they invited him to create a large mural for their new Abbey Grill extension, which opened in May 1968. The mural was painted over in the early 70s but I was lucky enough to find a picture taken just before the restaurant opened by local press photographer Brian Walker. For the first time in fifty years, we can get to see what John Michell had in his mind, right at the start of the modern ley revival, and it's exciting stuff.

The mural was, as John said later, "the first illustration of the St. Michael Line," depicted in all the freshness and glory of new discovery and replete with saucerological symbolism. The line was depicted as the figure's spine, with serpents twirling around it like a caduceus, "symbolising its vital energies." Hovering above the figure, like Horus over Hathor, was an Egyptian winged disc: the eye of Re. Saucer-shaped "chakra points" along the spine tell a story. The Piscean feet of the *Image* postscript have morphed into a kind of unfinned mermaid's tail, but a yin-yang symbol sits above St. Michael's Mount, where the Aquarian energy arrives and masculine and feminine are reunited. A labyrinthine serpent represents Glastonbury, astride the giant's midriff and the huge circle of Katherine Maltwood's Zodiac. Avebury was represented by a heart (it would be years before Glastonbury acquired the title of 'heart chakra'), while the eye, unfortunately out of shot, may have echoed the Eye of Horus: enlightenment in the east? Or perhaps surrounded by a sunburst, as in "The Eye of Heaven," featured in the coat of arms of the Suffolk town, very close to where Michell's family had lived during his own teenage years.

But it's the choice of gender that is really interesting. The figure, as John acknowledged, was "a reference to Blake's Albion," but Blake's Giant Albion was firmly male, held a sleeping prisoner by his own mind-forged manacles: "Jerusalem" was the female, sublimated 'Emanation' that would emerge when things went right again. By choosing to make his Albion female, Michell seems to have been suggesting that "Jerusalem" was indeed on its way. There are other resonances too. One medieval legend had it that Albion had been founded by Albina, the "White Goddess" herself, made famous

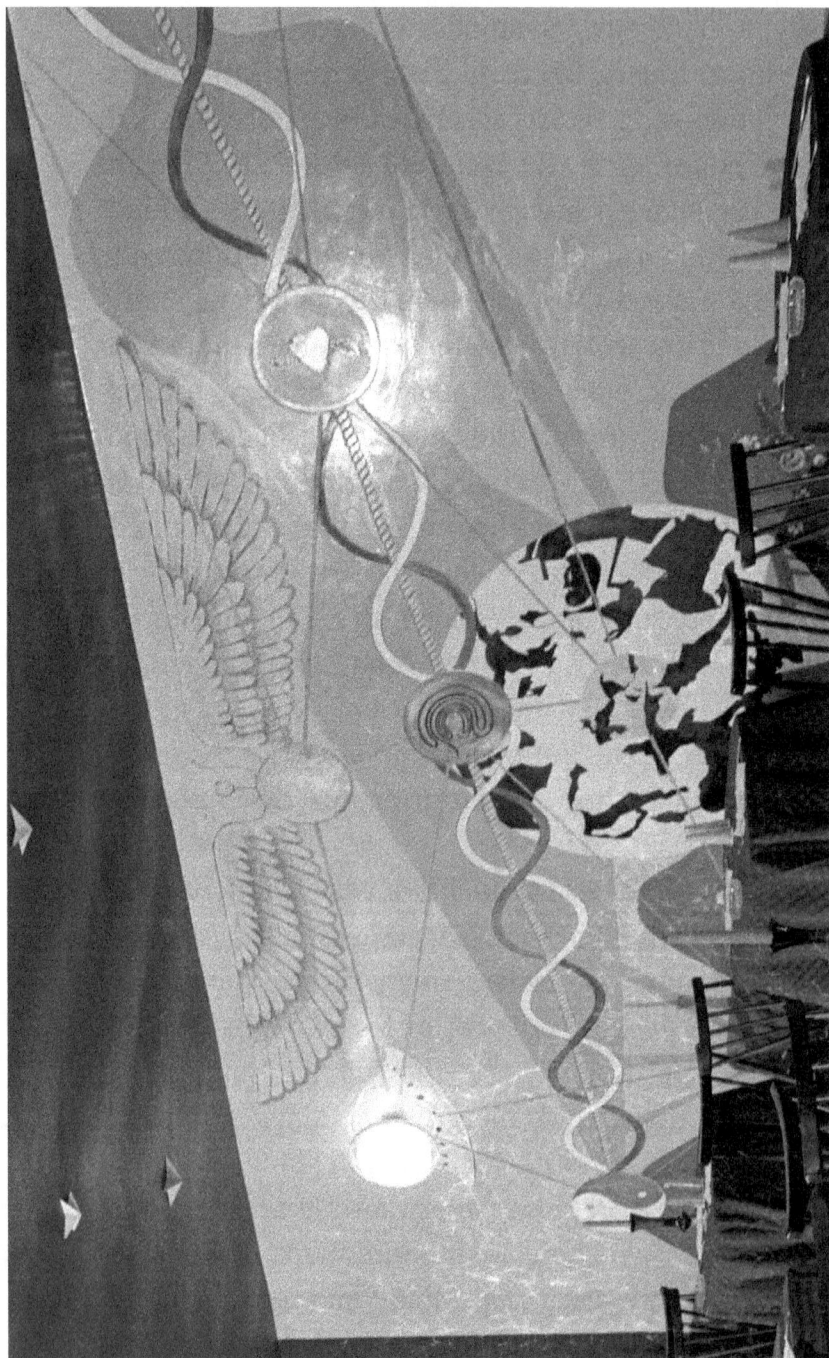

Albina and the Michael Line: John Michell's mural in the Abbey Cafe (Brian Walker)

by Robert Graves' book of that name, while her single eye in Eye conjures up *The Eye Goddess*, written by the archaeologist O.G.S. Crawford, which purported to find evidence of a goddess cult all around the ancient world. Both books helped to fuel the widespread Sixties belief that the universal religion of the ancients was built around a mother goddess. Albion/Albina thus stands in for the whole planet since, as Blake maintained and Michell was fond of quoting, "All things Begin & End in Albion's Ancient Druid Rocky Shore." John Michell's wide-hipped Albina was as female as Mother Earth herself.

LATENT POWER IN THE LAND

A week after his equinoctial revelation and all fired up, John Michell rang Bill Levy, one of the editors of the *International Times*, for whom he'd already published a synopsis of *The Flying Saucer Vision*, back in January when the world was a different place. "He is back in London after rural rides with Sir Mark Palmer and his gypsy band of horse-drawn caravans. Also, a side trip to Glastonbury. Wants to come over and tell me about it," wrote Levy in his diary. The result was another article for *IT*, appearing in October, called "Centres and Lines of the Latent Power in Britain." It was illustrated with images of the Glastonbury Zodiac and its relationship with the heavens, but sky-energies and messages were now firmly linked to the landscape itself: a not unexpected revelation, perhaps, from someone who'd been travelling at horse-pace along the green lanes of rural England. "The changes we are now experiencing are taken by some as leading towards panic and chaos, but to others they are the signal for a great liberation," he began.

> *This is a time of crisis, of questions yet unframed, old assumptions crumbling into a void, the new communication undeveloped. There can be no further progress in the old terms. The next step, whatever it may involve, a stage in evolution, contact with life from beyond the normal human vision, or the rediscovery of a lost source of inspiration on earth, can only take place in and where the genius loci, the native spirit, is still capable of being evoked … For just such a moment, we are told, the gods of Britain have been waiting, sleeping beyond the apple trees of Avalon, the spiritual twin of Britain.*

To Stukeley and Blake, "Britain lay under a spell, divorced from its gods, the old power forgotten. Yet Britain was the country destined to receive the new vision." The Druids, high magicians who "knew the land and the location of its centres of power and of the lines that linked them," had left clues that could be followed. Unlike, for instance, America, where native knowledge had been largely wiped out by colonisation, Britain had assimilated its successive invaders and consequently native tradition could be retrieved, perhaps with some chemical assistance: "Something of the meaning and potential power of the holy places can be felt by sharpening and expanding the senses while visiting these places." Arthur's knights "sought to preserve the arcane tradition and recapture its original purity. The Grail, the luminous vessel in the sky, in whose presence the mind became transcendent, was the vision they had glimpsed and strove to regain." This sounds like a pretty accurate description of Mark Palmer's questors, their aims and their erratic itinerary. "There is no known path through the country where the quest leads," John wrote, throwing down the mystical gauntlet for a generation of others to follow. The exhilarated Paul Screeton, future editor of *The Ley Hunter*, was one of those who responded: "Incendiary stuff! What a resounding clarion call."

CONFIRMATION IN THE SKIES

The 'gods of Britain' may have replaced the 'sky gods' of *The Flying Saucer Vision*, yet that October, even as *International Times* was at the printers, there was a major UFO flap in the West Country and the night sky was once more ablaze with portents. Whereas over the previous three years most UFO activity in the west had been concentrated around Warminster, this month "the Thing" was spotted near Glastonbury and Wells. The aliens were clearly tailing the Travellers, although it, or they, or who knows what, was or were seen by schoolchildren and policemen as well as hippies, and Questions were eventually asked in the House of Commons (no Answers were forthcoming). Michell, now back with the horse-drawns and parked up below the Tor, recalled how "we used to watch the nightly manoeuvrings of lights in the sky. Jung's prophecy of aerial portents being followed by a change in consciousness was evidently being fulfilled." They rang their friends and urged them to come down and bear witness, and among them was Craig Sams, macrobiotics pioneer, later co-founder of Green and Black's and in recent years dubbed 'the greenest man in Britain': "So here we are in the field, and up come the UFOs. We weren't tripping, I'd given up acid. I was completely normal, maybe I'd had a cup of tea about half an hour before. John Michell couldn't really see them very well because he's always been very short-sighted, Mark Palmer saw them, they were definitely there. They were in the classic cigar-shaped mother-ship form. Little lights emanating from them ..."

Michell's sight may have been short but his vision was clear and his star was certainly in the ascendant. As the publishing trade's house magazine *The Bookseller* noted, the publicity around the saucer-sightings "has proved most opportune for Sidgwick & Jackson," publishers of *The Flying Saucer Vision*, which hit the bookshops in November. Michell was interviewed on the regional TV news programme, and an appearance on the BBC was in the offing. The *Bristol Evening Post*

Mark Palmer and Maldwyn Thomas, camped up beneath the Tor in November 1967 (Brian Walker)

ran a two-page weekend special at the start of that month, illustrated with large photos of the photogenic Mark Palmer and Maldwyn Thomas.

Here
Come
The
Hippies.
The Hippies have moved into the West. Not just beatniks, not just unwashed layabouts – but genuine meditation-type hippies

readers were told. The intrepid journalist that interviewed them discovered that a great change was looming, a second coming of sorts, a manifestation of a new spirit. The "flower children" see Glastonbury as "the spiritual centre of Britain," on both Christian and pagan grounds – the Zodiac especially. Michell spelt out the three Lung Mei lines he'd identified, and in particular the line that linked the Michael sites, which marked the cult of the dragon, suppressed by Christian saints:

> *The rediscovery of the line of the great dragon of southern England and the fuller knowledge of its implication marks a stage towards the ending of the Enchantment of Britain, the achievement of the Grail and the reinvocation of King Arthur, the sleeping king who will awaken to restore the true spirit of Britain.*

Things had come a long way since he handed *The Flying Saucer Vision* to the publisher, as he told the *Sunday Times'* Pauline Peters when he turned up, very late, for an interview. "He finished the book a year ago and felt he had already developed beyond it," she said, accurately distilling his current thinking down to: "All leys lead to Glastonbury."

CHAPTER THREE

The Dragon in the Garden

EMBRACING THE DRAGON

"It seems that for many people the objects in the sky are linked with the features of the ground below," Michell told a ufology meeting in London in February, 1968. "UFOs are pointing towards a clue which in the past has been ignored by all but the most extreme visionaries – the revelations contained within the landscape itself." Quite literally. Flat-topped hills such as Glastonbury Tor had once been touched from the sky by "some fiery disc or coiled dragon that forever sanctified the hills to which it flew and the paths between them." The Tor is ringed by a series of terraces, which Tudor Pole, that other Merlin, claimed "may well conceal labyrinthine passages beneath." He postulated a role for these in pre-Christian worship: "Aspirants for Initiation who found their way through and up this maze emerged at the summit for illumination, but many fell by the way." John Michell amplified that vision, and made it more appealing to the acid generation. Initiation ceremonies, he suggested, may have involved *a journey underground and passage through a labyrinth, probably in a drugged and envisioned state. There are many native plants that could have been used to produce the necessary state of trance, and at least two of them grow on the lower slopes of Glastonbury Tor. At Glastonbury too, as on the slopes of many of the other sacred flat-topped hills, can be seen the remains of a great spiral labyrinth cut in the turf ... In the labyrinth was encountered some force, the full terror of which had to be experienced before those reaching the top were rewarded by the moment of enlightenment for which their years of training had prepared them. I believe that what they encountered was some manifestation of the force of which these hills are the natural conductor. And this force was known poetically as the monster or dragon within the labyrinth.*

Successful initiates "saw the lines of the current stretching away on all sides, across the country and across the world. They became attuned to a current of time which annihilated space ... The dragon power linked all men."

Part of a universal culture, the ancients perceived the world on a different scale to us. They left messages for people in a far-off future to discover and understand, in the form of monuments "of such staggering size and in such numbers that no amount of devastation could prevent them from delivering their message when men were again ready to receive." Michell

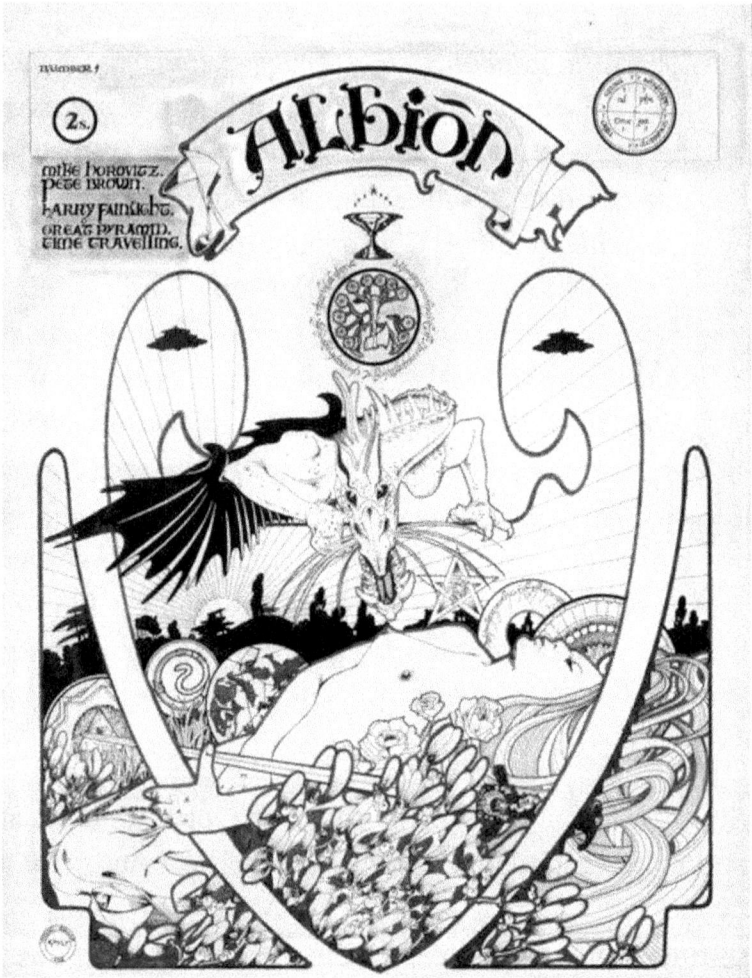

Michael English's cover design for *Albion* magazine, May 1968 (Victoria and Albert Museum, London)

praised the recent work of Alexander Thom, who claimed to have discovered evidence for a 'megalithic yard' and a high degree of geometric accuracy in the layout of Neolithic stone circles, but deplored the fact that Thom, "following the practice of archaeologists, is now working inwards" when he should have been looking outwards. Michell believed that such ancient monuments were themselves connected: "Stone circles were like the centres of great ripples spreading across the land, set out with perfect geometry on the face of the country, the radiating lines from one circle meeting those of another and dividing the country into vast crystalline shapes surrounding the sacred centres." Archaeologists, obsessed with detail, were unable to perceive this: "To see the message that *has* survived, we have to use the scale of poets rather than archaeologists, to look outwards rather than inwards" – poets such as Blake, who took the whole country as his theme (the giant Albion), or Maltwood with the huge zodiac; or Alfred Watkins and the ley system. Enter the Michael Line, the "most accessible and clearest defined of the English dragon lines." "The significance of St. Michael to this present time is that it is he who will announce the opening of the New Age," he wrote, echoing Tudor Pole. The older Merlin maintained that the shift between Ages meant movement out of duality and into unity. The younger one suggested that this might mean the end of good and evil. "St. Michael ejected Satan from heaven. It is he who one day must effect the great reconciliation" – "Satan" here equating with the dragon energies. Reconciliation between paganism and Christianity? A marriage of heaven and hell? Alchemy was at work.

The talk was published as "UFOs and the Message from the Past," as the centrepiece of the single issue of *Albion* magazine, which appeared in May 1968.

Another Notting Hill production, edited by one Steve Pank, Michell's article was probably the inspiration for the journal's name and certainly for the truly wonderful front cover, devised by Michael English, of silkscreen-poster pioneers and acidheads Hapshash and the Coloured Coat. References to the mural in the Abbey Cafe are very apparent, but English's lysergicised -orientalish-Blakeano-Tolkienic-art-nouveau-deco image is subtly different. The saucer-discs have come to earth in Avalon. The Eye of Horus, the serpent and the Zodiac, are scattered like giant puffballs or very magic mushrooms among the green fields behind the sleeping goddess, ripe for pollination, her breast as Glastonbury Tor. The Egyptian winged disc has become a fully-fledged red dragon, hovering like a lustful butterfly above her. It was the great reconciliation in action.

GANDALF'S GARDEN

Up at the World's End, where the King's Road kinked and the energies went haywire, opposite the striking facade of Granny Takes A Trip, stood Gandalf's Garden, a spiritual social centre for the turned-on generation that helped people make sense of the new consciousness. The founder was Muz Murray, who also edited *Gandalf's Garden* magazine (not to be confused with the *Guardian* newspaper, whose Jon Pepper described its colourful competitor as "a kind of Tolkienesque journalism"). Glastonbury was the central theme of Issue 4, which appeared in March 1969, and the main article was a five-page piece on the Zodiac, well-illustrated with maps and photographs. It was preceded by a highly exciting editorial, written by someone, perhaps Muz himself, who had digested Michell's own analysis and then transcended it:

> ... *could it be that at the intersections of the strange lines of psychic power, which appear to criss-cross our planet, certain forces accumulate and cause the landscape to arrange itself into meaningful designs, in much the same way as snowflakes and all other natural phenomena geometrically construct themselves? Such a cosmic concentration of energies could also have the property of subconsciously moulding the minds of the men who worked the land, causing them to create the Zodiac without being aware of it, since life on this earth is, in general, controlled by the subtle influence of the planets. Could the Zodiac be an immense symbolic landing stage marked out for the guidance of unearthly airborne objects, which even today still appear to use Glastonbury as a landmark?*

With that for an introduction, the piece itself would have to be an anticlimax, and so it was, despite the author's own description of the Zodiac as "The source of Glastonbury's mystique, the bubbling fount of all its legends ... Too Good to be True and Too Big to be Seen." The author was Mary Caine, proclaimed prophet-in-chief of the Zodiac revelation by the aforementioned *Guardian* three years earlier. Her *Garden* article leant heavily on the importance of poetic truth: "Archaeologists will argue; historians hiss; but why not try believing in the impossible for a change? The Red Queen in 'Alice' practised until she could believe at least six impossible things before breakfast. It's exhilarating. Anyway, it's a marvellous idea, and if it's not there, it ought to be. The Grey People will get you certified, but the map at least will be on your side." Alas, the map included several departures from Maltwood's original version, and Caine's piece drew a pained response in the next issue from one Elizabeth Leader, deploring Caine's "careless mistakes." A firm believer in the Zodiac "planisphere" (as she called it), which she saw as "a key to knowledge and sane communication," Leader believed that the priority must be to ensure that the site itself was preserved, which meant getting it officially recognised: "This can only be achieved by careful solid work, followed by tactful presentation to the planning authorities, and I would urge that all personal ambition for recognition as an 'expert' be shelved, efforts being concentrated on polite, persistent demand for a proper enquiry to be put in hand as soon as possible."

REFINDING LOST KNOWLEDGE

Uncoincidentally, Leader was herself engaged in just such an enterprise; indeed, Caine's article may have been a spur to it. Together with Janette Jackson, who like herself was a West London lady with Somerset roots, she was in the throes of setting up the Research into Lost Knowledge Organisation, which was formally founded in May of 1969, and attempted to woo an older and ideally more influential audience by operating as a respectable and properly-constituted organisation, worlds away from the laid-back gardeners at the World's End. Leader and Jackson had met at the home of Marjorie Von Harten, who with her sister Melissa Marston had just returned from a thirteen-year trek around the world tracing evidence of Gurdjieff's theory of 'legominisms', artefacts charged with hidden meaning by one culture for another to rediscover hundreds or thousands of years later. This was very much RILKO territory, and the two sisters became patrons.

Sacred geometry was at the heart of RILKO's work. In August 1969, just three months after its foundation, it published a well-illustrated if short collection of essays called *Glastonbury: A Study in Patterns*, paid for by Mrs Von Harten. The book was ostensibly aimed at planning authorities, landowners and others with archaeological clout to try and ensure statutory protection or at least fulsome excavation of all these sites lest lost knowledge be lost forever beneath modern development, reflecting widespread and growing dismay at the wholesale destruction of towns and cities during that rip-roaring all-change decade.

Three papers really stand out in the collection. One is Geoffrey Russell's *The Secret of the Grail*. A mystical experience involving a pattern of concentric circles "which had to do with the function of the brain" suddenly made sense to the author when he detected the same pattern in aerial pictures of the terracing around Tintagel and Glastonbury Tor. Like TP and John Michell, he saw the terraces as a labyrinth, with revelation ('the Grail') at the heart of it. This curiously neural metaphor on the face of it endorses Robin Carhart-Harris's contention that "hallucinating geometry is the experience of seeing the structure of your brain;" but Russell, claiming that Jung believed that "the world in our minds has no less reality either in substance or behaviour than the cosmic world around us," suggested that these labyrinths should be seen as an external representation of the internal spiritual quest, and investigated accordingly. As within, so without.

Arguably, RILKO's greatest achievement was to re-ignite interest in Frederick Bligh Bond, the Glastonbury Abbey archaeologist who had fallen foul of the authorities for claiming that his work had been guided from beyond the grave. His champions had included Marjorie Von Harten's father, Sir Charles Marston, a wealthy industrialist who had funded important archaeological excavations in the Near East and considered Glastonbury to be the "Jerusalem of the West." Keith Critchlow, an architect, later to become

Professor of Islamic Art and praised by Buckminster Fuller for his "vista-filling new realizations of nature's mathematical structuring," contributed a detailed geometrical survey of Glastonbury Abbey to the RILKO collection, and concluded that Bligh Bond had discovered "the significance and value of a buried science of cosmic harmonies, known in the past but virtually unknown to modern man." His findings did not stop at the Abbey precinct: "astounding implications" were likely to emerge from a fuller study of the "huge astronomical planisphere," the Zodiac, which, he claimed, "may turn out to be our greatest national heritage."

John Michell's contribution suggested that Glastonbury Abbey, like Stonehenge and other ancient sites, had been laid out on the "mystical ground plan" which Bligh Bond had discovered forty years earlier. A new ley line had been found, the Dod Lane ley, which ran from St. Benedict's Church, along the line of the Abbey nave, via the Tor to Stonehenge and on to Canterbury. Glastonbury and Stonehenge were thus connected by "a mercurial spirit path, the bed of an invisible stream along which the souls of the dead are conveyed on their passage to Avalon." The Abbey had been built as "the spiritual successor of Stonehenge, to exactly the same hidden plan as the monument on Salisbury Plan and for the same purpose: the distillation of solar energy and its fusion with the terrestrial current or life essence."

No mention here of UFOs or any kind of alien assistance, even though 1969 was the year of the Moon landing, and half the world was ecstatically embracing the Space Age. Michell had moved on, and his UFOs-in-the-past mantle slipped seamlessly to the likes of Erich Von Daniken, whose *Chariots of the Gods? Was God an Astronaut?* that year piloted the UFO firmly back into the nuts-and-bolts camp and away from hippy explorations of inner space. UFOs, though not totally absent, play a very small part in Michell's own book of 1969, *The View over Atlantis*, issued first as a short-run publication for subscribers and then, in November, launched onto a very eager public. Readers had to get almost to the end of the book to encounter flying saucers, whose movements were connected with "Druid magic," and, most significantly, whose appearance "is not entirely unrelated to the psychological condition of their observers." You need to be prepared, perhaps psychotropically, to see them. The emphasis now was firmly on terrestrial magic. Stonehenge and Glastonbury were built according to the same system of geometry, enshrining "the secret of a source of magical invocation inherited directly from a world of almost unimaginable antiquity," still visible in the landscape around Glastonbury, "laid out according to the magic square of the sun," and the key to which was to be found in the hidden geometry of the Abbey church. "The whole landscape of Britain has been laid out to a celestial pattern. Every hill has its astrological meaning, every district its centre of symmetry from which its hidden nature can be divined." It was a heady mix, and massively inspiring to the acid generation.

SPACED VISITORS

Meanwhile, back in Glastonbury itself and many geomantic miles from West London, the Schiraldis' Abbey Cafe and John Michell's mural were becoming a Mecca for hippy visitors and Atlantean souls – or perhaps a Crewe Junction. A *Central Somerset Gazette* article in April 1969, building on Michell's claim that flying saucers following ley lines converged on Glastonbury, dubbed the town "The Crewe of Flying Saucer-lines," and noted that his book had brought "a steady stream of flying saucer enthusiasts" to town ever since it was published. As Barry Miles recalled, "everyone seemed to be travelling to Glastonbury each weekend ... to seek the Holy Grail or plot ley lines. Other people waited patiently at Arthur's Tor for flying saucers to land ..."

The Rolling Stones were amongst them. Brian Jones came by in his white Roller, and Mick Jagger and Marianne Faithfull dropped into the cafe for tea a couple of times ("Nancy gave it to them on the house," recalled someone on a local Facebook page. Rock royalty doesn't buy its own tea). Mick and Marianne were among a group of UFO spotters whom John Michell took to the Tor that year. John had negotiated the sale of his family's Berkshire home, the well-named Stargroves, to Mick that April, which might have been a cue for that particular trip, but Mick was well into the whole 60s cosmic thing, as was Marianne too, "convinced there was a mystic link between druidic monuments and flying saucers. Extraterrestrials were going to read these signs from their spaceship windows and get the message. It was the local credo: Glastonbury, ley lines and intelligent life in outer space." Jagger actually installed a UFO detector at Stargroves: "The alarm kept on going off whenever he left home," according to Michael Luckman, "indicating the presence of strong electromagnetic activity in the immediate area," and presumably alienating the neighbours whether or not it succeeded in detecting aliens.

Other visitors included the Centre House Round Table who carried flares to the Tor-top one summer night, chanting mantras as they went: Centre House was another West London scene powerhouse, one of the first New Age spiritual centres with visiting gurus and wisdom-teachers from around the world, renowned for its healthy eating (Craig Sams ran the kitchen). But it was in 1969 that Glastonbury fever really took off, and some of it was down to Gandalf.

TOLKIEN AND THE GARDEN

At the start of the 1970s, an evangelical Anglican called Irving Hexham wrote a valuable if idiosyncratic fieldwork-based appraisal of the 'freak' community at Glastonbury as part of his Religious Studies MA at Bristol University. He looked in some depth at their mythology, from which it is immediately apparent that John Michell was one of the defining figures. Flying saucers were or were not extraterrestrial, they were synonymous with dragon energies, they followed ley lines. The natural power of the land had to be refound if humanity was to avoid disaster, and the freaks knew how to find it. As Colin Bord put it, in his review of *The View over Atlantis* for the Glastonbury community magazine *Torc*: "For one who has lain on the hills of England on a hot summer morning, and felt the surge and pulse of unnamed currents and forces flowing through the earth and across the country, this book contains truths that are beyond criticism."

Or, more truthfully, beyond everyday truth. John Michell had added something clearly precious to English mythology, much as J.R.R. Tolkien had done, and it's no surprise to find that Tolkien was another guru in the pantheon. Hexham's interviewees were all steeped in Lord of the Rings lore, and some even equated Glastonbury with the Shire: "They appear to believe that Tolkien had some 'special knowledge' when he wrote his story and that it is a true history of the pre-history of Glastonbury." Tolkien himself, by now an old man and often portrayed as being bemused or even affronted by his enthusiastic and unorthodox youthful following, actually gave his blessing to the Gandalf's Garden project and could be quite sympathetic to the hippy quest for colour and freedom, "inspired by admirable motives such as anti-regimentation, and anti-drabness, a sort of lurking romantic longing for 'cavaliers'."

Tolkien was amazed at the reception and influence that his books had had. "I feel as if an ever-darkening sky over our present world had been suddenly pierced, the clouds rolled back, and an almost forgotten sunlight had poured down again," he wrote. "As if indeed the horns of Hope had been heard again, as Pippin heard them suddenly at the absolute *nadir* of the fortunes of the West." These sentiments were precisely echoed in Muz Murray's 'mission statement', printed at the start of all six issues of *Gandalf's Garden*:

> *Gandalf the White Wizard … is fast becoming absorbed in the youthful world spirit as the mythological hero of the age, as graven an image on the eternal psyche as Merlin of the Arthurian legends. In the land of Middle Earth under threat of engulfment by the dark powers, Gandalf unites the differing races, mistrustful of each other through lack of understanding and communication, in a final effort to save the world. The crusader spirit in Gandalf is echoed in the cry of the Now Generation seeking an Alternative to the destructive forces of today's world, by spreading human love and aid, for the unity of all the peoples of the Earth.*
>
> *'Gandalf's Garden' grows in that same spirit. For 'Gandalf's Garden' is the magical garden of*

our inner worlds, overgrowing into the world of manifestation …

GANDALF BROADCASTING

Glastonbury had an important place in the magical garden. According to Muz Murray, "the tor and the giant Zodiac imprinted on the landscape round Glastonbury, which has had enough written about it now to hold some veracity, were together the centre of cosmic power in Atlantean days, and that at the present time there's an increasing influx of Atlantean souls on this planet, feeling foreign in a strange world, and seeking the centres where they intuitively feel the old powers of regeneration."

Gandalf's Garden did all it could to help them find their way there. Issue 4, which came out in March of 1969, quite explicitly urged people to get down to Glastonbury. A map showed the town as the pulsating heart of England, sounding out its name to the world. The contribution by 'Meiwana', a hash-like pseudonym surely, neatly combined the author's own post-Tudor Pole twist on Christianity with John Michell's notion of earth energies to be discovered by spiralling along the Tor ridges:

Jesus is the World Teacher, the Great Avatar, the Son of Man born and re-born from Age to Age under many names and he is active, as he has always been since the Fall of Man.

Those who turn to the Light, which is Truth, in meditation can hear his voice calling all who love peace to throng to his centre at Glastonbury; to take the pilgrim path, singing their way up the Tor, spiralling up from ridge to ridge, quite slowly, to draw the radiation up from the ground and to breathe in the blessing with the air that we may have the strength to take initiation ourselves, that is to die to the old, divisive, demanding ego and to be born into Freedom, Love, Wisdom and Joy.

Even more explicit was the remarkable contribution by Geoffrey Ashe, "Glastonbury: Key to the Future." Just four years earlier, when over twenty thousand Catholic pilgrims had been permitted by the Anglican authorities to process in the Abbey grounds, he'd suggested that Glastonbury was a kind of 'national shrine', and wondered if it might become "the scene of a fresh start for British Christianity; a temple of reconciliation;" but he came to realise that "the real re-awakening" was being wrought by the hippies, or "junior seekers," as he called them, discovering "Avalonian magic" via John Michell. "Britain will begin to be reborn when Glastonbury is," he told the *Garden* readers.

The Giant Albion will begin to wake up when his sons and daughters gather inside that enchanted boundary, and summon him with the right words, the right actions, a different life. Pilgrimage? Yes,

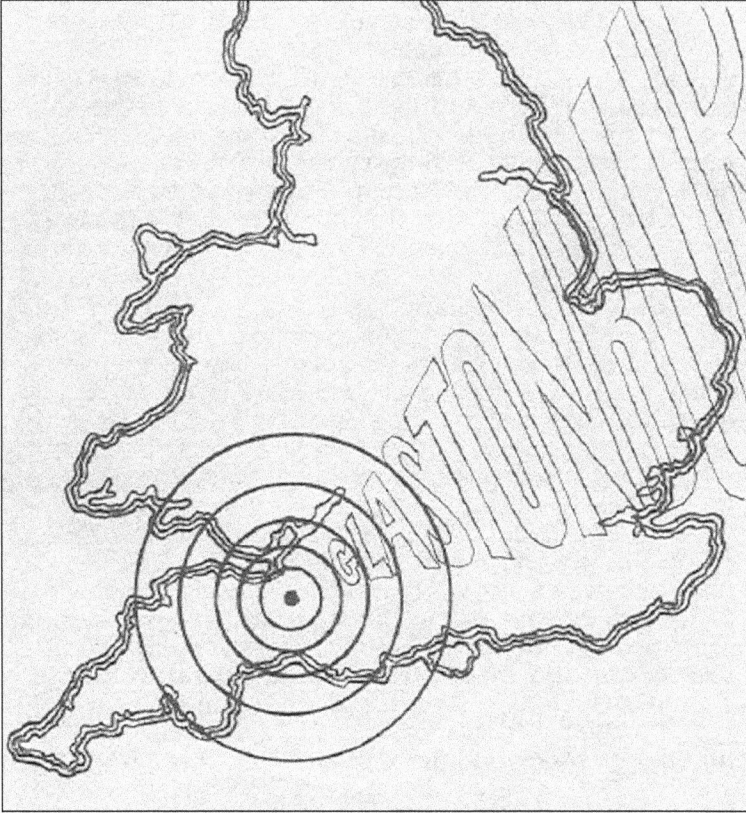

Glastonbury Calling (*Gandalf's Garden*, March 1969) (Muz Murray)

but more than pilgrimage – an enduring community of Avalon, with a constant coming and going, a heart stirring the blood into motion again. The time to found that community is drawing closer.

THE HIPPIES ARRIVE

And they came. It was as if, as Gary Lachman puts it, "the spores from *Gandalf's Garden* had been blown in

Flower Power in the High Street: Pat Leyshon's shop (Brian Walker)

by the wind and taken hold." According to Barry Miles, "There was first a trickle, then an exodus of people from Chelsea moving to the West Country to study the Glastonbury Zodiac, the ley lines and to hunt for traces of King Arthur," but it was not just from Chelsea that they came – or even London. On Whit Sunday, at the end of May, the Chalice Well experienced "a minor invasion of hippies," whose rowdiness was ascribed by a Trustee to their ignorance; they came from "near slum quarters in the Midlands and knew very little of beauty ... Something had touched them at the Chalice Well and their frivolity and bad language were merely a sort of shy, bashful withdrawal from the reality of spiritual being." Ah, those coy Midlanders.

A few weeks later, seeing the writing on the wall, Glastonbury shopkeeper Pat Leyshon painted bright giant flowers on hers, to the consternation of the Town Clerk. "Flower Power Hits the High Street," carolled the *Central Somerset Gazette*. In those pre-motorway days, all the traffic came through town, and the shop became very well known. Mistaking symptom for cause, the locals blamed her for bringing in the hippies. By August, it was being reported that " 'hippies' have taken over Glastonbury Tor as a summer retreat," and the *Gazette* guessed that they'd be central to the gossip at September's Tor Fair: "What with strange objects in the sky over the Tor, flower power being brought to the town high street, and the convergence of colourful hippies camping just outside the town, they will have plenty to talk about."

An article by Jon Pepper in the *Guardian* at the very end of that year and decade testifies to the scale of Glastonbury's recent hippy influx:

> *The frosts and fogs have come to Avalon. The deep, brooding mysteries still cling to the vale, even more so in the present melds of haze and wintry sunbeams, but the 1969 Children's Crusades to Glastonbury in search of the town's strange enchantments have finally ended, defeated by the cold. The fields are now empty of their tents and flutes. The place has sunk into a thankful hibernation.*
>
> *Glastonbury has had a remarkable year. Hundreds of young people – hippies, poets, mystics, weirdos and sundry unclassifiables – have hitchhiked and tramped into the town from all over Britain,*

Europe and even America since March looking for 'vibrations'.

Word of the vibes, emanating from the belief that Glastonbury is to be the centre of a new British civilisation, sensitive and learned, joyful and co-operative, has travelled persistently along the grapevines of both the Underground (Straight Hippie) and Overground (Occult and Mystic) worlds of the young who, in their great colourful hordes, have now made Glastonbury a modern Mecca for Aquarian pilgrims.

Jan Oakley was one such 'Overgrounder'. An astrologically-minded teenager from Essex, she'd bought the OS maps covering the area of the Zodiac, put them on her bedroom wall and traced out all the figures. She came to Glastonbury on a camping holiday with friends. "When I got off the coach, I had a strange feeling like I'd come home, and that's never left," she says. She gave up home and job and moved down, and half a century later she's still there. It was not just the Underground or the Overground grapevines that brought people in though. Some simply read about the place in the straight press, as Irving Hexham discovered. Brendan Lehane's article in the *Telegraph* magazine at the tail end of '66 had been read by "a number of freaks" and also, allegedly, by Mark Palmer and his "London socialites," whose rejection of materialism and pursuit of "spiritual peace" later hippies were aware of and sought to emulate. Others first heard about Glastonbury through the reports in the *News of the World* about "the drug scene there," which goes to show that there's no such thing as bad publicity.

BACK TO THE GARDEN

They came full of idealism, fired up by the magic of the place. "We were drawn by an exciting sense of something new and fantastic happening here," says Bruce Garrard, who first came to town at the same time as Jan Oakley and has been active on the scene ever since. BBC West made a surprisingly sympathetic TV documentary called *Trip to the Truth* about the hippy pioneers. First screened in January of 1972, although some of the interviews took place many months earlier, a copy of this gem, buried uncatalogued in the BBC archive, was discovered and retrieved through the efforts of Anthony 'Legolas' Mawson, another of the 69ers. The producers allowed people to describe what drew them to Glastonbury without too much external prompting, and in the comfortable surroundings of the Abbey Cafe they used Christian terminology to explain how it worked: "You have to abandon yourself to God and go where he says," we are told; in the same way that animals are drawn naturally to stone circles, "so are we – naturally." When the time comes, we'll maybe disperse, but for now "we've all got to come together."

This apparent aimlessness concealed a very practical desire amongst some to build the alternative society in the place that had been preordained for it. Mark Palmer had wanted to buy land "not just in Glastonbury but everywhere that flower children gather, so that they can establish colonies to make everything they need and grow all the food they want." Others were more focussed on the town. Patrick Benham, an important figure in the 'New Glastonbury Community', came to the town in '69, wanting "to get back to human-scale forms of living, to rediscover a sense of *real* community and *real* communication ... Glastonbury seemed just the place where the 'alternative dream' might achieve a measure of realization." Anthony Mawson "passionately believed that there was a real possibility/opportunity for change in the social order to a more caring/sharing society, and in Glastonbury, at the outset, that was actually happening. We were forging a new way of being together, few had money, but whenever we got any it went into a pot in the Abbey Cafe to help pay for feeding everybody!"

Building the New Jerusalem within the constraints of a pre-existing town was never going to be an easy call, but to begin with local reception to the new arrivals was pretty good-humoured. For one thing, as the *Bristol Evening Post* observed, "Glastonbury is accustomed to strange visitors from all parts of the Western hemisphere." The Brotherhood of the Essenes made an annual pilgrimage to the Tor, and when the Druids came in 1964, a month after Rahtz' dig had begun, the mayor greeted them at the Tor-top in

Legolas (Anthony Mawson) and friends in the Abbey Cafe, explaining the lure of Glastonbury to the BBC.

appropriately mystic fashion: "Glastonbury, with all its historic associations and this hill on which we stand, in particular, holds many mysteries which even now are being sought after. May it be that if and when they are revealed, these ancient truths may be an inspiration to us all in these modern times." Welcoming Druids to a ritual on a hilltop was not something that the average small-town mayor was called upon to do, but the locals were proudly aware that their town was a bit different.

It also helped that Glastonbury wasn't the back of beyond. Young people here were as attuned as young people in any small town to the music of the day. Pikes Records in Northload Street prided themselves on selling the latest releases as soon as they came out, while Brian Mapstone's legendary Saturday night dances in the Town Hall attracted people from all over the county to hear such names as Elton John, Jethro Tull, Fleetwood Mac, Tyrannosaurus Rex, and (the week before the Chelsea crew arrived) Long John Baldry; in November '67 the psychedelic band Paper Blitz Tissues performed there, advertised as 'flower power' in the *Gazette*. It followed that a lot of local youngsters were sympathetic to the new arrivals. In October, 1969, a local team won a youth debate with the proposition that "hippies are the only people who have discovered an ideal way of life." And some young locals *were* hippies. Scorpio Bickerstaffe, a teenager from Wells, six miles away, was hitching with a friend down to Glastonbury sometime in 1967 when Brian Jones pulled up in his Rolls-Royce. Such things happened in those days (and apparently Brian used to send his chauffeur off to a hotel while he himself dossed down beside the car: these were egalitarian times). He took the two lads down to Mark Palmer's encampment at Charlie Cottrell's farm on Cinnamon Lane, just below the Tor. Mark and Maldwyn were very friendly, shared gear and food and ideas; "they put me on the path," says Scorpio.

The newcomers found a really warm welcome from older folk of the Avalonian persuasion scattered around the town and thereabouts. Christine Jagge and Elsie Hartshorn from the Winds of Truth sanctuary in Ashwell Lane, for instance. "I love the hippies, I will do anything to help them," Christine told the *Trip*

✷ **GLASTONBURY TOWN HALL** ✷
SOMERSET'S TOP SATURDAY DANCE

SATURDAY, SEPTEMBER 16th   Admission 7/6

DIRECT FROM LONDON THE FANTASTIC

LONG JOHN BALDRY!

With **ALAN WALKER, STEWART A. BROWN, MARSHA HUNT and BLUESOLOGY!**

Plus Yeovil's Blues Band **THE GENERATION!**

NEXT WEEK   THE GODS! + THE KYND   5/-

to the Truth team. "They would serve tea and Tartex sandwiches in their garden after a weekly séance on a Sunday, and gave small teachings in which we were warned about not losing sight of our souls' purpose by damaging our temples with drugs," recalls Francis Deas. "It was too late for some!"

Francis was another who'd heeded the call in *Gandalf's Garden*. He'd actually been selling the magazine, alongside the *International Times*, around his home town of Stafford, and came to Glastonbury one summer's day in 1969. "I climbed the Tor and spent a pleasant few hours chatting to other young pilgrims, or 'freaks' as we sometimes called ourselves, those who had been drawn to this numinous place,

John Shelly, wearing one of the ceramic hearts he gave to new hippy arrivals

with all its mystical associations. As evening drew on and I walked down the 'hill of vision', I had left it rather late to find somewhere to camp for the night, so thought I'd knock on the door of a wooden house called Chalice Orchard." The house had once belonged to Dion Fortune and was now the home of a well-known potter called John Shelly, who lived there with his wife Betty. Shelly had been heavily involved in Peter Caddy's Glastonbury Foundation initiative and, even though it came to naught, remained massively inspired by the town and convinced of its spiritual importance: "this place will be like an iridescent pearl of flame," he wrote to Caddy, "gleaming and glowing like a pulsating sun on the earth's surface. All will feel and come to this spark of Heaven and take its light in their eyes to every corner of the world and send others in an unending flow til gold is covering all the earth and I am you are you are me and we are everyone and everyone is us ..."

Shelly was an enthusiastic supporter of the hippies, "the angelic generation," as he described them in another BBC TV feature on Glastonbury in September, 1970: "The grey people think they're bad people but they're not, they're good people." He presented new arrivals with ceramic heart talismans of his own making, inspired by Dion Fortune's famous book (*Avalon of the Heart*). "He felt that the arrival in the town of the young hippies was a welcome sign of the dawning of Aquarius," recalls Francis. "I think most of us had pretty anti-materialist attitudes and John seemed to fulfil the role of a hierophant who validated our spiritual aspirations and ideals ... but 'angelic' would be stretching it a bit."

That first evening, Francis knocked on Shelly's door to ask for water: "He filled my water bottle and asked me a few questions about why I had come to Glastonbury. I told him that I'd had a strong intuition that I should come as soon as I had read about the place. I had a sense of certainty that my destiny, my independent life was to begin here, but I wasn't sure in

Francis Deas (*top left*) and friends at the cottage in Barton St Mary on the zodiac sign of the Dove (Libra), soon to become the Dove Centre, a pioneering craft community (Francis Deas)

what way. John replied rather enigmatically by saying 'we've been expecting you,' which was a surprise to me. Of course, I wasn't really sure who <u>we</u> were but it was nice to be welcomed, and after further conversation I was invited in to eat a supper of bread and cheese off a wooden plate in their living room. Betty brought me an earthenware mug of herb tea. Amongst other things, I learned that John was a skilled earthenware potter; to my eye almost everything in their house was either beautiful or useful or both – it made a strong impression on me."

FEAR OF ULLAGE

But some locals, far too many of them, took against the hippies from the start. A month before the New Age missionaries set out from London, a local councillor called for organised resistance to the spread of hippy culture: "There should be a national appeal to the people of the realm to uphold the morals of the British." The police swooped on the September travellers almost as soon as they arrived, found drugs in Camilla Drummond's car and charged five of them. John Michell and the Raineys were bailed at £15 each, but Camilla and Luiz Saldanha went to court, where they outraged the prosecution by professing "the rightness of everything they do." They were fined heavily because the sentence had to be exemplary: "The moral conscience of the country is involved."

Scorpio Bickerstaffe, looking soulful for the BBC.

Hence perhaps Michell's description of Glastonbury as "stubborn" in the postscript to the *Image* article, written days later. Awakening the giant goddess was going to be a challenge. The early hippies were thought to be wealthy – a cartoon in the *Gazette* tellingly suggested that only hippies would be able to afford to buy posh new houses in Glastonbury – but Mick Jagger was allegedly turned down when he put in a bid for a house in Chilkwell Street. Mark Palmer had wanted to buy somewhere on the Mendips with an orchard, grazing for horses and a view of the Tor, and actually enquired about a farm near Priddy, but it was sold over his head, or that's what Palmer believed. Not even wealthy hippies were welcome in the countryside (he regularly returned to Glastonbury all the same, though later describing himself as a 'horse dealer' – a considerably more rugged moniker than 'flower child', and perhaps a safer one, though Francis Deas, who looked after his horses for a spell, says that he still looked the part: "He had a stylish gypsy look, with a hint of woodsmoke in the bright scarf").

At one point, the travellers' barrel-tops were rolled by rednecks. Thanks to press photographer Brian Walker, they found sanctuary with his family in Benedict Street, and Scorpio's got fond memories of the scene that developed there. Honk, the bassist out of the Graham Bond Band, was a visitor, and someone else who carried Tim Rose's 'Morning Dew' apocalyptic single in his pocket like a talisman. They played it all the time:

> *What they've been saying all these years is so true.*
> *They have chased away all our morning dew.*

All over the Western world, young people were flooding out of the cities in pursuit of morning dew while it still existed, and the old guard were nervous. "We've got to get ourselves back to the garden," sang Joni Mitchell of Woodstock and its unexpected half-million visitors in August 1969. With the example of Woodstock no doubt in their minds, local Somerset bigwigs reacted to the announcement of the Bath & West Blues Festival in

1970 by closing down anywhere around Glastonbury where festival-goers might stay. When Jan Oakley first landed in town, she'd camped like many others on the Tor, on Chalice Hill, in the Abbey Barn (which was still a barn then), "hiding in plain sight," to the consternation of the authorities. Jan had first heard about Glastonbury from a friend who went to a local boarding school called Millfield; now the headmaster put the Tor out of bounds to the boys because "we do not like their way of life." The National Trust banned camping on the Tor, with local chairman Colonel Gould dismissing hippies as "useless ullage." Worst of all, the Chalice Well gardens were closed for the whole summer because the Warden found the new breed of visitors offensive: "These people are not hippies in the spiritual sense, they are tramps." When the gardens were finally reopened, a charge was introduced to keep the great unwashed at bay.

WELL AND ILL

Washing was a big issue. Jon Pepper singled out the Chalice Well trustees' "paroxysms of righteous horror" at the fact that the Well's "holy, healing waters have apparently been used for communal ablutions. Of course, the intruders cannot do anything right: half the town accuses them of being unwashed and an affront to civilisation, while the other half berates them for washing their jeans, shaving, and sprucing up in the Well waters." You have to wonder what Tudor Pole himself would have done. Although he was setting the scene for the start of the New Age in August 1967, his concern at the "invasion" of flower folk a few weeks later was a tad unpromising. But over the next few months, he seems to have warmed to them, and at least one took it upon herself to make contact with him directly. Margaret Russell, the twenty-one-year-old daughter of his old friend and patron David Russell and part of the Raineys' 'coterie' (TP's word), decided for reasons best known to herself to write to the eighty-three-year old seer and "extol the great benefits she has received from LSD and from smoking marijuana." He wasn't convinced, and probably wrote back to tell her that drugs were not necessary to get high in Glastonbury, since he thought that the "attraction to Avalon and Chalice Well by so many youngsters who belong to the Beatles and similar groups" was an unexpected result of the anti-drug movement. His grasp of youth culture may have been shaky, but his words demonstrate that young hippies were certainly being drawn to the Well in numbers. He sympathised with those who lamented this new-found "intrusion by the general populace" but was also pleased by it: "Evidently the time has come when 'all things' hidden are to be gradually brought out into the light of day." Just a couple of months before he died, he was hoping that Lord Harlech, head of the newly-founded Harlech TV franchise, would make a half-hour programme about the Well. "Our hallowed site is filled with the Spirit of the Christ and with the ideals of Chivalry and Fellowship symbolised by the visionary splendour of the Holy Grail," he told the Companions that August. Lord Harlech was Jane Rainey's father. Were these words partly aimed at the Raineys and their ilk, in the hope of catching father's eye? The programme was never made; imagine how many more flowery grail-questors would have been attracted if it had been!

But Wellesley Tudor Pole died in September, 1968, and the Chalice Well Trust went into what Sir George Trevelyan was to tactfully describe as "a delaying period … The time was not yet right for forging ahead" – the Trustees did not know what they wanted and the Warden knew that he certainly didn't want hippies. Which was a shame, because the mystery of the Upper Room was a major draw for them. When Irving Hexham came to town, he found that the mere existence of the Upper Room was seen by the freaks as evidence that Christ was going to return to Glastonbury. The Warden's hostility simply fanned their curiosity: "They persist in trying to find out more about it and in telling stories about it. Thus, its very existence has become one of the great attractions which Glastonbury holds for the Freaks." A curious note in the Chalice Well archives, dated August 1970 and signed by TP's two surviving sisters, declared that: "We the undersigned feel that, although we called the Cup the Holy Grail in 1906, we now prefer to call it the Sapphire Blue

Bowl" – was this perhaps prompted by concern at how seriously the Chalice Well mystery was being taken by the youngsters at the gate?

TP believed that Chalice Well water had real healing powers. In his last months, he began to practice distance-healing from the Upper Room and, shortly before his death, went public with a recommendation that the waters should be administered in small doses, "about seven drops diluted in a glass of water, milk or fruit juice." Fairly precise echoes here of the miracle cures that had drawn thousands of people to the town in 1751. Back then, the wealthy ones had been welcomed as harbingers of a possible spa, but most of them were not wealthy at all. They camped out in the fields and ruffled local feathers, to the extent that one "surly Peasant" threatened to poison the waters, and the local authorities tried to ban "poor Persons" from entering the town. Now the wheel had come round full circle, although to begin with the numbers were a fraction of what they were in 1751. Most of the hundreds who came in '69 went home again, and between Christmas of 1970 and Easter of 1972, Irving Hexham estimated that there were on average no more than 25 "Settlers" and up to 30 "Visitors" in the town – "Visitors" being defined as folk who stayed for no more than three weeks and slept rough, often on the Tor. "Settlers," on the other hand, had lived here for at least six months, though they were often pretty nomadic. "Quite a few seem to go to London during the coldest part of the winter," he noted; to Notting Hill particularly: no surprises there. Most of the Visitors came from middle-class backgrounds, were grammar school educated, and included a smattering of art school dropouts. The Settlers, on the other hand, were older, from less well-off backgrounds, and lived mostly "in old caravans which they park on the sides of roads leading out of the town."

In March, 1971, the police launched a dawn raid on a small hippy settlement by the abandoned railway station, and forcibly moved their caravans to roadsides where the danger from redneck violence was greater. A couple of weeks later, airgun pellets were fired at caravans, and in June skinheads threw bricks at them, hospitalising one resident. More and more shops and cafes in town put up "No Hippy" signs, with smelly clothes being given as the usual pretext. It was all a long way from Mark Palmer's crushed yellow velvet. Plans to set up a vigilante group and "remove the hippies, tents, caravans, the lot" were abandoned on legal advice: "I was amazed by the irrational hatred exhibited by some apparently well-educated and otherwise intelligent people," wrote Hexham. In the face of so much hostility, the extraordinary thing is that so many of them stuck it out.

CHAPTER FOUR

The First of the Festivals

CLASS PLAYERS

According to Hexham, around a hundred people stayed in the fields around Glastonbury during the weeks before the 1971 Glastonbury Fair, or 'Fayre' as it was mistitled in the film that Nic Roeg made. The festival's first incarnation at Worthy Farm, Pilton Pop in 1970, had nothing whatever to do with Glastonbury and its mythos. Michael Eavis had been inspired by June's Bath Blues Festival just up the road at Shepton Mallet – in the other direction from Glastonbury – and it was pure coincidence that his farm was in sight of the Tor. Nothing in the literature or in the online accounts suggests any sense of a link to Avalon. Did any of Glastonbury's hippies turn up? It'd be surprising if they hadn't, but if they did then they must have seen it as a trip out of Avalon and not into it, an excursion into the wider world of festivals.

The main man behind the 1971 festival was Andrew Kerr, who came from the same well-heeled echelons as Mark Palmer and John Michell, with whom he'd once lodged. He too lived in Notting Hill, and he was

Andrew Kerr in exuberant mood (Brian Walker)

close to the height of Cool – Jimi Hendrix once leafed through his record collection, ye gods, and he arranged for Marianne Faithfull to meet (or 'be introduced') to Princess Margaret, the slightly rebellious royal. He'd led a double life as Randolph Churchill's secretary, working on the massive official biography of his famous father, and had come to be quite friendly with Randolph's daughter Arabella, who was being groomed for a life in high society that she didn't want. Expected to become a NATO pin-up, she refused and fled to Somerset to help Andrew with the festival, notably with public relations: the Churchill connection undoubtedly helped in winning round the locals. Privileged game-players perhaps, but there are twists to the class system that often go unnoticed. Quite apart from the many well-born rebels who've walked away from their destined expectations to fight for social justice, the system that takes bullies to the top makes many victims. Rich losers, and not-so-rich ones, like Andrew Kerr, bullied and mocked both at home and at school for what was only later diagnosed as dyslexia, well-connected but not wealthy, poor relations to rich families. Randolph Churchill was insulated against failure and opprobrium by his extraordinary surname, but yet was also conscious of the impossibility of living up to his father, doomed in the end to write the old man's biography. Perhaps he recognised a kindred spirit in Kerr. Anyway.

Kerr, released from his Churchillian duties when Randolph died in 1968, became more and more involved with music and festivals. Like Eavis, he crept into the Bath Blues Festival through a hole in the fence and, like Eavis, was very inspired by it. He went to the Isle of Wight Festival in August, but was depressed by its commercialism and resolved then and there to put on a free festival at an ancient sacred site. Much smitten with *The View over Atlantis*, he considered but rejected the possibility of a site near Stonehenge on practical grounds, and instead went for Glastonbury, the site that John Michell deemed to be Stonehenge's spiritual successor. Kerr missed Pilton Pop but immediately afterwards contacted Eavis, who not only said 'yes' but gave him his blessing – and his farmhouse to live in. A fortnight after Pilton Pop, Worthy Farm was taken over by hippies planning to stage a full-on hippy festival the next year. Things happened fast that summer. Eavis's trust was remarkable, but it's also true that he needed the money. Pilton Pop had lost a bundle – he was paying off Marc Bolan's fee from the milk cheque for several months – and he hoped the London hippies' event would cover the rest of the debt (ha!).

Twelve thousand people turned up to Glastonbury Fair: a respectable crowd, though still tiny in comparison with Woodstock, or the Isle of Wight, or even the Bath Blues Festival; but its significance has been enormous, and as Andy Roberts says its roots were "deep in the counter culture and closely linked with LSD. Had it not been for the psychedelic focus of the first major Glastonbury event, the festival in its present form would not exist." Kerr, who'd been an acid head for some time, was one of those who saw the creation of LSD in 1943 as the antidote to the atom bomb, its discovery providential; as paraphrased by Hexham who interviewed him in curiously Churchillian terms "When men were most lost, when they discovered the most terrible weapon available to man, then too they discovered man's greatest spiritual aid."

SPIRITUAL ENGINEERING

Geomantic magic underlay the whole event. It was a conscious attempt to apply John Michell's theories of prehistoric science, and both organisers and audience were steeped in it. A visiting *Guardian* journalist noticed that *The View over Atlantis* was "a sort of Gideon's Bible at the Fair," freely available and found everywhere. Michell claimed that William Blake had aspired to "the recreation of the old system of spiritual engineering, whose ruins are still evident in every corner of the country." The Blake connection is a tad implausible, but that word 'engineering' is very intriguing. Michell had long been fascinated by the ruins of Britain's Industrial Age communications, the canals and branch-line railways which had been abandoned wholesale and now formed marginal spaces where marginal people of all kinds could hang out and even, like the folk at Glastonbury Station, squat. In a fascinating aside to his 1967 *Image* article, Michell pointed out that these linear no-man's-lands, which served as "a sort of lateral sanctuary ... for a submerged portion of the human population," might eventually form routes for "distinctive lines of thought across the country." Dragon folklore had travelled along the Lung Mei in this way; maybe all manner of other ideas and concepts could travel like this too. The ley system was a network for the Underground.

"Worthy Farm in Somerset is linked to Stonehenge, the Glastonbury Zodiac and the great cosmic pattern

Pyramid of Light – Paul Misso's celebrated photograph, used for the Glastonbury Fayre triple album (Paul Misso/IDEA)

of ley lines and energy points. The whole system is a mind-bender," wrote Kerr, who himself dowsed John Michell's Glastonbury-Stonehenge ley as it ran across Eavis's fields, and found the "spiral of reactions" which was chosen as the spot for the first of the famous Pyramid Stages. The night before Kerr's meeting with Eavis, he met stage designer Bill Harkin on the Tor with a group of friends, and no doubt sacred substances were shared. Harkin had had some powerful dreams about a pyramid-shaped stage, and Kerr gave him the go-ahead to build one that followed Michell's ideas on sacred proportion. He consulted both Michell and Keith Critchlow, applied their findings from the geometry of Glastonbury Abbey, and came up with a scale model of the Great Pyramid of Giza. The idea, according to Kerr, was to "draw to it beneficial astrological influence into our tired planet. We hoped that people would go away feeling a lot better for the experience, more creative, happier and more appreciative of the Universe, not in a heavy way but proving that life is really a gas." It worked. When John Michell died in 2009, Eavis was one of the mourners. "John set me up, really," he said, which was true enough, but let it not be forgot that Kerr's merry band of hippies were the ones who actually woke the sleeping dragon and bathed her in beauty. As Andrew told the festival audience from the stage, "The Earth is groaning for contact with our ears and eyes."

CHRISTING THE EARTH

People forget how much that first festival was a consciously spiritual event ("pop-mystical," Geoffrey Ashe called it). Though not a Christian himself, Andrew Kerr couched his sentiments in conventional Christian terms when he tried wooing the Pilton parishioners before the event:

> The aims ... of Glastonbury Fair are not to make money but to make the people who come more aware of what goes on in the countryside, to make them appreciate it and realise the importance of preserving it. If God's laws are observed, His nature respected, and His gift of Life honoured, the new generation

will live on a happier Earth. The time is overdue for a genuine spiritual awakening.

For all the long hair, strange clothes and peculiar habits, the section of the younger generation known as hippies for the most part are striving for such an awakening. They find that society on the whole, in their opinion, has lost its way.

He cultivated the Pilton vicar, who likened Kerr's crew up at Worthy Farm to the Benedictines, which "was kind but in some respects not particularly true." There was quite a lot of religion at the event itself. There was a Jesus Tent, with ecumenical services in which Catholics and Protestants took turns; there was Taizé singing, as well as various non-Christian celebrants – Muz 'Gandalf' Murray opened the event by leading a chant, the Sufi teacher Pir Vilayat was there, and Guru Maharaji, aka Prem Rawat of the Divine Light Mission, turned up unexpectedly. Kerr was serious about his spiritual engineering, and though his description of the Pyramid Stage as "the first sacred building to be erected since the Reformation" was not calculated to soften Anglican hearts, he was still disappointed that no-one in power saw what he called "the true meaning of the event." The local MP, supportive at first, decried Kerr's "plagiarism of Christian religion." Kerr was indignant. "How could it have been? The event had partially Christian roots"…

Well, partially. "What we were trying to do was to stimulate the Earth's nervous system with joy,

The wings of Horus over a fiery Tor. Image by an unknown artist for the Glastonbury Fair Manifesto, 1971

appreciation and happiness so that our Mother Planet would respond by breeding a happier, more balanced race of men and women, animals and plants. It was a fertility rite." The notion that fertility and goodwill were linked was derived from Findhorn, whose founders claimed that music had helped restore the place's soil fertility (not that they would have approved of Glastonbury Fair. When Francis Deas visited Findhorn soon afterwards, he found that they "had very judgmental views about the very music that was also an expression of changing consciousness. They viewed it as low-vibrational and forbade it to be played in the community"). But Glastonbury's freak community, according to Hexham, were in no doubt that the Fair had "prepared the area around Glastonbury to receive Christ." John Shelly told him that the event "might be the occasion of Christ's return and was certainly an indication that the return was near."

Francis, who was then Arabella Churchill's boyfriend, recruited Shelly as a respectable local elder to write a spiritual spin for the "Glastonbury Fair Manifesto", which is well worth repeating:

> *Humanity has become a cold, hard crust upon the surface of the Earth through which nothing can pass. At the moment, we are doing this planet no good.*
>
> *The Earth creates us out of herself and of herself. We are the very flower of all her produce and she makes us for a very special purpose. That purpose, which we are not fulfilling, is to feed back into the Earth through ourselves that 'Nectar' from the gods 'out there'.*
>
> *The Earth is starving and dying for the want of spirit food. Great powers of this food are drawn down when young hearts come together in joy, relaxed happiness, freedom and nature-like conditions; enhanced by singing, music, dancing and, above all, love.*
>
> *This Fair is unique from its very inception.*
>
> *It is willed by God.*
>
> *At this special time – on this special place – 'The holyest Erthe in England.' And the Earth will be replenished. Miracle conditions will be created so that God's spirit can and will flow through the hearts of the young angelic generation in order to 'Christ'*

the Earth. That is one of the great duties of Man and that is what the young are about to do for Him here in the 'Heart Centre' of England – Glastonbury.

THIRD WAY OUT

Christ's imminent return was the immediate reason many freaks gave Irving Hexham to explain their coming to Glastonbury. What people actually meant by that was a lot less clear. Some identified Christ with King Arthur; others with Gandalf, "the avatar of the New Age … a Christ figure who represents goodness." Others were expecting a literal return of Jesus of Nazareth. Christian symbolism is much apparent in the caravans into which the *Trip to the Truth* film crew were invited. "I'm waiting for the Second Coming," Christine Chapman told the programme. "Great Britain has led the world as a nation and they will do so again when we wake up our souls to Jesus Christ and know that he's coming back." She was echoing Tudor Pole's less-explicitly Christian aspirations for the Chalice Well, and his conviction that "the people of our Island will be given the opportunity once more to lead humanity out of its present darkness into the Light." And, as John Shelly told the nation, "All the wonderful things that are to be will start here in Glastonbury … a spiritual and intellectual revolution will spread from here throughout the land, and from this land throughout the world."

Note, yet again, the sense that Britain had a special role to play in the world, and that Glastonbury held the key to a better way of British being. Hippies were as prone as their elders to feeling the malaise of Britain. We jaded twenty-first-century schizoids look back with nostalgia for the confidence, colour and the sounds of the Swinging Sixties and a simpler age, but that's not how it seemed at the time. The straight world wasn't exactly brimming with inspirational choices, what with Vietnam, and the Soviet invasion of Czechoslovakia, and the Chinese Cultural Revolution sullying the once-hallowed pages of Chairman Mao's *Little Red Book*. The student revolution of May '68 in France was crushed; a month earlier, right here in Britain, Enoch Powell made his still-notorious 'Rivers of Blood' speech urging an end to black immigration. Where were the people of conscience to look for hope and inspiration? Back, out, in. Tolkien, Glastonbury, the landscape, the mythological past. Conventional politics were finished. "Already politicians and their world seem remote and irrelevant," wrote John Michell in January '67, mischievously invoking Lenin for the politically-minded readers of the *International Times* as an unlikely prophet of the New Age; in similar vein, Allen Ginsberg, soon after his visit to Arthur's tomb in Glastonbury in 1966, wrote off both left and right and instead declared that "Blake's idea of Jerusalem, Jerusalemic Britain ... is now more and more valid." Five years later, Hexham was surprised to find his freaks steeped in Arthurian nationalism: "He is the past and future king. At his coming, Britain will be restored to her former glory. Arthur is the spirit of the British race; and when he returns, spiritual values will once more rule our land." By 'British' they meant 'Celtic', however, not the Britain of more recent centuries, responsible for so much bad karma in the world. The New Age/ Second Coming had a redemptive quality to it, the chance to start again. "For the Freaks the promise of a New Age which will eradicate the remnants of an unhappy past is a great source of confidence. They see themselves as the children of the New Age and heralds of its coming."

Unsurprisingly, the three writers who contributed to the *Gandalf's Garden* Glastonbury special shared the anti-imperial view of Britain and its future. Geoffrey Ashe, with his characteristic optimism, once described the British withdrawal from India and thereafter everywhere else as a conscience-driven reaction to Mahatma Gandhi: "In response to Gandhi, Britain resigned a world mission which had outlived whatever rightness it had, and turned back to a humbler and saner quest for self-realization." Mary Caine, in a letter to Katherine Maltwood's widower, thought that the Zodiac was the product of an earlier, deeper, better Britain, associated with "our profound sense of mission, and our destiny, now so sadly forgotten and covered over with inadequate and misleading interpretations. These, when exposed in all their hollowness (our Empire-building, our public school system of education, etc.), leave us stripped of all reason for our still-persisting sense of greatness, and purpose." Properly understood, she believed that Maltwood's theory "could have a profoundly therapeutic effect on our sick and bewildered national self-respect and restore at a deep level our sense of direction, as a spiritual leader and diviner for the world – not as a military or economic power."

Neither of them laboured these points in their *Garden* pieces, however. The national redemption angle was left to 'Meiwana', whose contribution began with the rousing words to *Jerusalem*, explicated as a divine message: "Blake wrote the words of this poem as they came to him from beyond. It was a case of automatic writing, Blake being but the medium through which the message was transcribed." An enigmatic verse then follows:

> *Five stars move over Glaston Tor*
> *In the Holy Isle, the off-shore Isle,*
> *In the cold, grey glitter of the northern seas.*
> *Britain is the isle, the cold-shouldered isle,*
> *Where some now ask*
> *and the Heavens reply.*

"Cold-shouldered" by whom? By Europe perhaps? Early in 1967, the Foreign Secretary George Brown urged the German Chancellor Willi Brandt to help Britain join the Common Market "so that we can take the lead," but the French had no desire to cede leadership of Europe to Britain, and vetoed the application. Politically cold-shouldered, Britain's leadership vocation clearly belonged to higher realms, as it had been in the days of Christ, according to 'Meiwana', who had had a direct encounter with the etheric Jesus at Chalice Well: Christ had been initiated as a Druid at Glastonbury, "then the purest centre of learning on Earth." She might have got this idea from John Michell's October 1967 *IT* piece, which claimed that in ancient times "Britain was known on the Continent as the sacred land, the gateway to the incorporate world … As Avalon was to Britain, so were these islands to the rest of Europe. Just what this means is something we no longer know, something we must discover before any further advance can be made."

ENGLISH REDEMPTION SONG

Um, er, yes, well. Europe came and went, and the British shoulder is proudly cold again. Half a century later, on the other side of Brexit, is there any hope for the dream of Glastonbury and Albion? We're still floundering in the wake of empire, still struggling with notions of superiority and national distinctiveness that truss us up in knots. But there are some good things too. The NHS for one, which, try as they might, the money-men have failed to destroy completely. Glastonbury Festival is another.

The British used to be famous for their uptightness. Way back in 1934, J.B. Priestley had deplored the lack of colourful events that offered some "grand release from ordinary reality": "Let us have, not only for fun but for sweet sanity's sake, some great popular festivals, some day of universal high jinks, as an escape from the growing pressure or monotony of our ordinary lives." It took a while, but that goal at least has been met – and in the process, alternative England found a place in the mainstream. As George McKay insightfully says, Glastonbury Festival is all about "the reconstruction of alternative traditions of Englishness." It is a curious fact that there were no more official festivals at Worthy Farm until 1979. The Festival only really started kicking in after Thatcher came to power, and during the 1980s it became one of the major foci of radical resistance. During those critical years of nuclear rearmament, the festival was the main source of income and publicity for the revitalised CND, which the same J. B. Priestley had co-founded in the 1950s (leading the way in nuclear disarmament would reclaim an appropriate role for Britain, he'd declared in 1957; it would be "the first step in reviving the soul and spirit of the British people"). In 1984, that Orwell-fateful year, CND spokesman and my favourite historian E.P. Thompson, at Eavis's invitation, made a speech from the Pyramid stage: "This has not only been a nation of money-makers and imperialists, it has been a nation of inventors, of writers, of activists, artists, theatres and musicians." Looking directly at the assembled crowds he told them: "It is this alternative nation which I can see in front of me now." Thomas H. Green identified the festival squarely with the 1980s counter-culture – it may no longer have been trendy but "it still hummed with energy, woven with something bawdy, ancient and rustic." And as Banksy says, it "throws mud in the eye of common sense and market forces. It shouldn't really exist, never mind succeed."

When the first festival was being set up in June of 1971, a visiting journalist from *The Observer* described it as "one of the weirdest events ever staged in modern Britain." It is a measure of how far things have come since then that this weird event is now as much a feature of the British summer calendar as Wimbledon. The Festival has changed a lot of course, to endless cries of sell-out (and Banksy once put up a sign saying: "Queue here to complain festival is not as good as it used to be" – it seems nostalgia is endemic at Pilton). Old heads look back at the trashing of the travellers and the break-up of the free festival scene as the end of a truer dream, and in some ways of course it was. But Glastonbury Festival, and the myriad of paid-for events that it has spawned, has opened the eyes of so many people who'd never have gone anywhere near a "Peoples' Free Party" of the kind we used to put on for our own ilk alone.

Andrew Kerr and Arabella Churchill learned the hard way that there's no such thing as a free festival, but the outpouring of support after the event, most notably in musicians contributing to the 'Glastonbury Fayre' triple album, redeemed the situation and on the way helped to confirm the mystique of that first festival as The One; perhaps helped by the fact that there were no more official 'Glastonburys' until 1979. Yet in recent years, the festival organisation has been quite systematically downplaying the '71 event; which is a shame because it's completely unnecessary. Is it because of the hippies, or the drugs ... or the relative non-appearance of Michael Eavis? No-one disputes the genius, sincerity and tenacity of Eavis in making a success of the greatest show on Earth, but his good-intentioned efforts to get involved in that first festival were rebuffed until late in the day, when practical savvy was needed to make it a reality. Eavis is nowhere to be seen in Nicholas Roeg's documentary film of the festival: "We've got the farm!" says Bill Harbin, gleefully, to camera, quoting Andrew Kerr. The farm, note, not the farmer. The debts were finally paid, and Kerr was invited back by Eavis to help site-manage the festival between 1979 and 1986, pioneer turned foreman. Role reversal, even: sweet revenge? Toff come unstuck. But it was also a highly productive partnership, in some ways the realisation of the dream of returning to the green and pleasant land: at last, a countryman with land and dedication and commitment who shared the basic dream, which was to propagate peace, love and harmony, rather than making money, which is why the festival has worked so well for so long.

And it's still got a radical edge. Jeremy Corbyn's appearance on the Pyramid Stage in 2017 was his biggest and best-attended rally. He gave the alternative nation an alternative view of how Britain could be, if only we could rise like lions from our slumbers. The fact that we couldn't is another and more woeful measure of our inability to let go of the crap and reinvent ourselves; but in some ways, the country has moved towards the festival too. The festival is huge, way too huge, but it has contributed just as hugely to the loosening-up of some nasty national knots. Like an enormous flying saucer, it lands on the fields of Pilton Park each year and creates another reality; and never forget that it all began with a bunch of tripped-out hippies.

Well, I dreamed I saw the silver spaceships lying
In the yellow haze of the Sun.
There were children crying and colours flying
All around the chosen ones.
All in a dream, all in a dream.

CHAPTER FIVE

Madly Wrong or Madly Right?

THE GREAT HIPPY FREAK-OUT

Hippy fashion went out fast. In 1971, the former Hung On You shop at 430 King's Road was taken over by Malcolm McLaren and Vivienne Westwood, scornful of the likes of Marianne Faithfull and the Kinks, Michael Rainey's former patrons who nonetheless still crossed the familiar threshold in pursuit of what was new; or rather, the new sort of old. The soft medievalish Sixties garments were long gone; instead, they flogged an older horse and sold Fifties rocker stock for a couple of years before morphing the shop into Sex, selling shock and mockery; from this the Sex Pistols shot out and punk was born. It was the first post-modern boutique. "Modernity killed every night," read the sign over the door. Any time but the present for the avant-garde. The new wave washed over, Thatcher came along and the shop at the World's End went apocalyptic. In 1980, McLaren and Westwood installed a giant clock outside the shop with a thirteen-hour dial. It's still there now, though the clock ticks swiftly backwards. The future has been and gone.

Time running backward at the World's End

Away beyond Chelsea, hippies and punks drifted uncomfortably into each other, fused and tried to build a new world on the roads as Mark Palmer had done, though these New Age Travellers were demonised and their festivals suppressed. Not that many of them would have bought the 'New Age' tag, which was foisted on them by the media. No-one these days likes to be called 'New Age'. People talk about it like something severely dated, an embarrassing phase we went through, a clichéd fashion statement. The Age of Aquarius, like the future, has been and gone. But has it? Is the New Age really broken? So much of what was once called New Age is now mainstream.

The 'genuine meditation-type' people who seemed so exotic to the journalists of 1967 are now to be found everywhere, for instance – and that's just the therapy end of the hippy package. So much else that seemed so outlandish then, from caring for the Earth to caring about what we eat, has become common knowledge as humanity scrabbles around for the last of the morning dew. So were the hippies right about reality too?

END OF THE LINE

Cynics, especially local ones, claimed that Glastonbury Festival cashed in on the good name of that small town, seven miles away from Pilton where it takes place. Now the tables are turned. The festival is so gigantic and its fame so widespread that many people in the wider world are surprised to discover that there's a town of that name at all. But there is, and it is still New Age Central; and though it still struggles with its identity, the town's high street is one of the busiest high streets in the country (and, as Scorpio Bickerstaffe points out, in its own way as exotic now as King's Road was in the 60s). The festival brings in millions to the Somerset economy too. There's gold in them thar dreams. Real reality has been created, the one with money signs attached.

Not that reality's what it used to be, of course. A recent article in *New Scientist* looked at quantum physicists' "attempt to resurrect reality" and concluded that "we can't consider reality to be made of real objects, only real relations." This reminds me of Dion Fortune's 'lines of psychic force' that survived even after the power-centres they'd once linked had been disconnected. If the pathway's the thing, the connection, might there yet be room for the old straight track in the quantum universe?

November 1969 saw the renewal of *The Ley Hunter* magazine, and the publication of *The View over Atlantis*, and the start of the Earth Mysteries quest which set thousands of people on the ley-hunting trail, looking for a deeper ancient land beneath the corrupted and compromised veneer of modern Britain. The Michael Line (which, as purists point out, is more of a 'corridor' than a line, stretching miles off true in order to take in all the sites that have been claimed for it) ended up exacerbating a major split in the ley-hunting world between those who were determined to try and prove the physical existence of the ley in scientific terms to allay all doubters, and those who refused to be contained and restrained by such definition and preferred to go on their own intuition. The scientifically-inclined gave in; they could not find the hard evidence that they wanted, and pronounced the ley line dead. The other lot are living the dream. A dowser, Hamish Miller, travelled the Michael Line with earth-mysteries writer Paul Broadhurst and detected lines of energy that wove, caduceus-style, around the central line like the snakes in Michell's now-obliterated mural, with gendered energies they dubbed Michael and Mary. Their book, *The Sun and the Serpent*, first published in 1989, is probably the most successful book about ley lines ever written, and has given birth to a small industry of long-distance ley-making at a time when people are really getting into long-distance walking for the good of body and soul and the soul of the planet. Whether or not ley lines used to have any objective reality is beside the point; they've certainly got one now. John Michell once called his dragon-lines "distinctive lines of thought across the country;" they're now becoming pilgrimage routes, ritualised by use, ways for people to walk, ponder, reorient and above all play. Those earth dragons are joyful, playful things, fluid and mobile, like dolphins or dogs. They respond to interaction; they like it when people want to play with them and dream that the energy's flowing again. The Glastonbury Zodiac is just the same. Did it exist before Katherine Maltwood came along? Does the answer really matter? It definitely exists now, and peoples' lives are transformed through experiences they have had through spending time in it. These things are as real as you want them to be.

ACID ARCHAEOLOGY

From the "vast crystalline shapes" of John Michell's Albion landscape to the self-constructing snowflakes of the *Gandalf's Garden* editorial, hippies found it easy to believe that there was an underlying symmetry to the ancient landscape, testifying to the awareness and skills of ancient monument-builders who were aware of the Earth's geometry and built harmoniously and in accordance with it. These visions owe much to LSD, and it's no coincidence that the fascination with sacred geometry was so strong in the Sixties.

Archaeologists tore their hair out over the direction in which John Michell sent the nation's youth. A generation later, by which time the charity shops were full of discarded copies of *The View over Atlantis*, up popped Julian Cope, whose acid-inspired understanding of hoar antiquity spawned his best-selling *Modern Antiquarian* and another tranche of landscape mystics. The indifference of Spiral Tribe's Mark Harrison to earth mysteries was shaken when he discovered acid: "Suddenly, all that changed," he said, and this defining 90s sound system went on the road, fired up by what Andy Roberts calls "the native British spirituality." I'm not sure about that phrase myself, but I have to say that acid took me that way too. I have had very similar experiences, occasionally on acid but more honestly as a consequence of the change in consciousness my few trips had wrought. I have felt the hillforts hum with green-gold energy, I have stood on the eye of the White Horse on a September dawn and felt the utter rightness of those ancient artists' lines and curves, and none of my book-learning has dispelled that. It's statistically curious that so many acid heads find themselves drawn to mystic prehistory and the ancient places. Ultimately, it's why I became an archaeologist – and probably why I didn't stick at it. My studies took me as far as relativism, the insights into the nature of truth and knowledge production broadly labelled 'post-modernism' (a label which these days is about as popular as 'New Age', used mostly by opponents to denigrate; nobody likes to be boxed), formulated by agile thinkers on the European mainland whilst British intellectuals were still confidently being modern. British anti-intellectual alternative types went pre-ancient instead of post-modern. It tickles me that *Albion* appeared in May '68, the month that France went crazy. The hippy rebellion was of a very different kind, but in its own way almost as profound.

The vision of an ancient age of harmony and understanding is pure wishful thinking, archaeologists tell us. The human past is messy and always has been; there was no Golden Age, no era of shimmering perfection. But maybe it's our time-frame that's at fault. Maybe it is simply too attenuated, too human-centric. Most of us still struggle with supranational identities, let alone suprahuman ones; but in truth, the hierarchy of nested identities is infinite. We are mammals, we are living creatures of the Earth, we are children of the Universe, we are stardust and golden and eternal. Species come and species go. Planets come and planets go. Galaxies likewise. The Universe is one eternal pulse, making and breaking, new galaxies and black holes, balanced and ordered. Viewed cosmically, from the perspective in which galaxies form and disintegrate in harmonious and predictable sequence, humanity's attempts to impose its own chaos on the Universe seem a bit ridiculous. And if, as the quantum people tell us, time is just a construct, the vision of ancient harmony is the vision of future harmony too. By re-writing the ancient past, we also right it – setting up the chess-pieces for the next game in the cosmic cycle. If that's not far out, what is?

References

Introduction

Ashe, Geoffrey "Glastonbury: Key to the Future" *Gandalf's Garden* #4 (March, 1969) p15.

Benham, Patrick *The Avalonians*. Glastonbury, Gothic Image (2006, second edition).

Garrard, Bruce *Free State: Glastonbury's Alternative Community 1970 to 2000 and Beyond*. Glastonbury, Unique Publications (2014).

Vonnegut, Kurt *Bagombo Snuff Box: Uncollected Short Fiction*. New York, G.P. Putnam's Sons (1999) p10.

The Mad Kings Road

Faithfull, Marianne *Memories, Dreams and Reflections* London Fourth Estate (2007) pp150–1.

Levy, Shawn *Ready Steady Go!* London, Fourth Estate (2002) p266.

Miles, Barry *In the Sixties*. London, Jonathan Cape (2002) p232.

Moraes, Henrietta *Henrietta*. London, Hamish Hamilton (1995) pp92–3.

Walsh, John "The Wild Sloanes who Made the Sixties Happen" *Tatler* online (posted 21st June, 2017).

CHAPTER ONE. *Jerusalemic Britain*

Glastonbury Tamed

Benham, Patrick *The Avalonians*. Glastonbury, Gothic Image (2006, second edition).

Fenge, Gerry *The Two Worlds of Wellesley Tudor Pole*. Everett, WA, USA, Starseed Publications (2010).

MacNeice, Louis "Autumn Sequel" from Canto XXII in Peter McDonald (ed): *The Collected Poems of Louis MacNeice*. London, Faber and Faber (2007).

Stout, Adam *Glastonbury Holy Thorn: Story of a Legend*. Newlyn, Green & Pleasant (2020).

Stout, Adam "The Onset of Avalon" (talk for Glastonbury Antiquarian Society, 2015) https://glastonburysite.wordpress.com/talks/the-onset-of-avalon/

Stout, Adam *The Thorn and the Waters: Miraculous Glastonbury in the Eighteenth Century*. Frome, Green & Pleasant (2007).

Arthur Returns

"An Historic Day for Roman Catholics at Glastonbury. Statue Unveiled by Apostolic Delegate to Great Britain" *Central Somerset Gazette* (15th July, 1955) p1.

Ashe, Geoffrey "Arthur and English History" in Ashe (ed): *The Quest for Arthur's Britain*. New York, USA (1968) pp225–43, 241–3, 253.

Ashe, Geoffrey *King Arthur's Avalon*. London, Fontana (1973, second edition) p7.

Ashe, Geoffrey *Miracles*. London, Abacus (1978) pp180–1.

Carpenter, H. and Tolkien, C. *The Letters of J.R.R. Tolkien*. London, Allen & Unwin (1981) pp250–1.

Gilchrist, R. "Sacred Myths: Archaeology and Authenticity" in Gilchrist, R. *Sacred Heritage: Monastic Archaeology, Identities, Beliefs*. Cambridge. Cambridge University Press (2020) pp176–218 (p186).

Hexham, Irving *Some Aspects of the Contemporary Search for an Alternative Society*. Unpublished M.A. Thesis, University of Bristol (1972) p55, n31.

Hollis, Christopher *Glastonbury and England*. London, Sheed & Ward (1927) p10.

Lindsay, Jack *Arthur and his Times*. London, Frederick Muller (1958) p283.

Trevor, Meriol *The Last of Britain*. London, Macmillan (1956) pp230–1, 442.

The Chalice Well Gateway

"Archaeologists Draw a Blank" *Bristol Evening Post* (25th August, 1966) p11.

"Beckery Chapel near Glastonbury 'Earliest known UK Monastic Life'" (5th December, 2016) https://www.bbc.co.uk/news/uk-england-somerset-38187299

Fenge, Gerry *The Two Worlds of Wellesley Tudor Pole*. Everett, WA, USA: Starseed Publications (2010) pp94–100.

Fletcher, Paul *Light upon the Path: The Unpublished Writings of Wellesley Tudor Pole*. Glastonbury, Chalice Well Press (2022) pp47, 97–9, 136–7, 167–97.

Gaythorpe, E. (ed) *My Dear Alexias: Letters from Wellesley Tudor Pole to Rosamond Lehmann*. Jersey, Neville Spearman (1979) pp133–4.

Rahtz, Philip "Glastonbury Tor" in Ashe, G. (ed) *The Quest for Arthur's Britain* (1968) pp139–154 (pp140–1).

St. Michael and the Tor

anon (W. Tudor Pole) (ed) *Michael Prince of Heaven: Captain of the Angelic Hosts – With Reference to the Special Associations of St. Michael with Cornwall*. London, J. M. Watkins (1951).

Caddy, Peter *In Perfect Timing: Memoirs of a Man for the New Millennium*. Findhorn, Findhorn Press (1996) pp149, 157, 307, 323–6, 329–30.

Fenge, Gerry *The Two Worlds of Wellesley Tudor Pole*. p155.

Firth, Violet (Dion Fortune) *Avalon of the Heart*. London, F. Muller (1934) pp97–8.

Firth, Violet (Dion Fortune) *The Goat Foot God*. London, Williams & Norgate Ltd. (1936) p89.

Fletcher, Paul *Light upon the Path*. pp90–2, 117 (and n12, 208–9, 220–1, 312–3).

Gaythorpe, E. (ed) *My Dear Alexias: Letters from Wellesley Tudor Pole to Rosamond Lehmann*. Jersey, Neville Spearman (1979) pp51, 71, 141, 160, 200.

Mikaal, The Lord (Chavarinis) *The Winds of Truth and the Yanihian Script*. Glastonbury (1978, ninth edition) piv, 83 (n70, 77–8).

Mikaal, The Lord (Chavarinis) *The Testament of Love*. Glastonbury (1966) p6.

Pugh, Liebie *et al The Michael Power of Glastonbury.* Universal Link, St. Anne's-on-Sea (1965).

'Summer Pilgrimage to Iona', *The Churches' Fellowship for Psychical Study Quarterly Review* 35 (Mar 1963) p8.

Unidentified Flying Zodiac

Barber, John "England, Wake up to Wonderful Gift, says Researcher." *Bristol Evening Post* (17th March, 1965) p10.

Caine, Mary "1961–1962 Letters Between Mary Caine and John Maltwood" online at: https://victoria landscapezodiac.wordpress.com/2017/11/18/ 1961-1962-letters-between-mary-caine-and-john-maltwood/

Chalker, Bill "June Marsden: Alien Sirens Come Calling" (2021) online posting at: https://theozfiles.blogspot. com/2021/02/june-marsden-alien-sirens-came-calling.html

Goddard, Jimmy *A Life of Ley Hunting.* Diary entry: "The Pendragon Party (12th November, 1966)" online at: http://www.jimgoddard.myfreeola.uk/leyhunt/ lhunt66.htm

Heselton, Philip *Tony Wedd: New Age Pioneer.* Hull, Northern Earth Mysteries (1986).

Jung, C. *Flying Saucers: A Modern Myth of Things Seen in the Skies.* London, Routledge & Paul (1959).

Lehane, Brendan "Did Christ Come to Britain?" *Telegraph Weekend Magazine* No. 116 (16th December, 1966) pp43–6.

Maltwood, Katherine *A Guide to Glastonbury's Temple of the Stars*. London, James Clarke (new edition, 1964).

Moorhouse, Geoffrey "Temple of the Stars" *Guardian* (25th January, 1966) p9.

Stout, Adam *Creating Prehistory: Druids, Ley Hunters and Archaeologists in Pre-War Britain*. London, Wiley Blackwell (2008) pp173–214.

Trench, Brinsley le Poer *Men Among Mankind*. London, Neville Spearman. pp23–4, 31–41.

Watson, Edward "Farewell Pendragon: The Pendragon Society 1959–2009" (article dated 2nd May, 2009) online at: https://clasmerdin.blogspot.com/2009/05/farewell-pendragon.html

Transformation

"Gone: A Man who offers Big Returns" *Sunday Mirror* (16th August, 1964) p2.

Colman, Beth "When the Warminster 'Thing' Terrorized a Small English Town" (posted 8th Dec, 2020) online at: https://www.mentalfloss.com/article/638338/warminster-thing-ufo

Kerr, Andrew *Intolerably Hip: The Memoirs of Andrew Kerr*. Kirstead, Frontier Publishing (2011) pp88–9.

Michell, John, Introduction to Miller, H. and Broadhurst, P. *The Sun and the Serpent*. Launceston, Pendragon Press (1998, fifth edition) pp11–8.

Michell, John "Alien Infiltration", lecture to unknown audience (21st May, 1966) online at: https://archive.org/details/UFOLOGYAPrimerInAudioUKAUS19461989 Guide

Michell, John "A New Kind of Energy" in J. Mackay (ed): *Michellany: A John Michell Reader*. London, Michellany Editions (2010) pp33–4.

Nicholson, John "The Time of the Signs" in *An English Figure: Two Essays on the Work of John Michell* London: Bozo 1987 p27.

Roberts, Andy "A Saucer Full of Secrets" *Magonia* #87 (February, 2005) online at: https://magonia magazine.blogspot.com/2014/01/a-saucer-full-of-secrets.html

Roberts, Andy *Albion Dreaming: A Popular History of LSD in Britain*. London, Marshall Cavendish (2008) p73.

Rhone, Christine "The Work of John Michell: Visionary Ley Hunter, Author & Mystic Philosopher", talk at Megalithomania conference (2023) online at: https://www.youtube.com/watch?v=sbYeZYRtxW0

Screeton, Paul *John Michell: From Atlantis to Avalon*. Avebury, Alternative Albion (2010) p96.

Trench, Brinsley le Poer *Men Among Mankind*. pp71–3.

Blake, the Beats and the Birth of the New Age

Ashe, Geoffrey *King Arthur's Avalon*. p286.

Clark, Tom "Knights of the Road", in *London Review of Books* Vol. 22 No. 13 (6th July, 2000) online at: https://www.lrb.co.uk/the-paper/v22/n13/tom-clark/knights-of-the-road

Green, Jonathon *Days in the Life*. London, Pimlico. pviii.

Ginsberg, Allen "The Art of Poetry" from interview in the *Paris Review* #37 (Spring, 1966) online at https://www.artsalve-productions.eu/literature/Allen_Ginsberg.html

Hagan, Jade *New Age Romanticism and the Afterlives of William Blake.* Unpublished PhD thesis, Rice University (2019) (p99, online).

Michell, John, Introduction to *The Sun and the Serpent.* p11.

Michell, John *The Flying Saucer Vision.* London, Sphere Books (1974, second edition) pp22–3, 30, 156, 161–4, plate xiv.

CHAPTER TWO. *1967*

Beautiful Inside

Cleave, Maureen "Metamorphosis of an English Boy" *Evening Standard* (2nd March, 1967) p8.

Cohn, Nik *Today there are no gentlemen: The changes in Englishmen's Clothes since the War.* London, Weidenfeld and Nicolson (1971) pp93, 119–20.

Michell, John "Summer of the Upper Crusties" *The Tatler* (November, 1989). Reprinted in Mackay (ed), *Michellany.* pp38–44.

Michell, John *The Flying Saucer Vision,* pp18, 22–3.

Screeton, Paul *John Michell: From Atlantis to Avalon.* Avebury, Alternative Albion (2010) p6.

Journey to the Centre of the World

"Queen's Former Page Boy on a Drugs Charge" *Cheddar Valley Gazette* (13th September, 1968) p3.

Atagong, Felix "A Tale of Two Henriettas" (20th March, 2020) posted online at https://atagong.com/iggy/archives/2020/03/a-tale-of-two-henriettas.html

Faithfull, Marianne with Dalton, David *Faithfull: An Autobiography*. London, Michael Joseph, (1994) pp65, 87–8.

Faithfull, Marianne with Dalton, David *Memories, Dreams and Reflections*, pp150–3.

Luckman, Michael *Alien Rock: The Rock 'n' Roll Extraterrestrial Connection*. New York, Pocket Books (2005) pp57–8.

Michell, John "Summer of the Upper Crusties" from *The Tatler* (November, 1989). Reprinted in *Michellany*. pp38–44.

Morton, H.V. *In Search of England*. London, Methuen (1927).

Roberts, Andy *Albion Dreaming*. p92.

Walker, N. "Men will Think Pink" *San Francisco Examiner* (5th Sept, 1967) p27.

St. Michael and the Dragon Line

"Essenes Forecast 'Second Advent'" *Central Somerset Gazette* (30th June, 1967) p9.

"Flower Group Probe Secrets of the Tor" *Bristol Evening Post* (18th September, 1967) p21.

"Flower People Seek 'The Truth' in Glastonbury" *Central Somerset Gazette* (22nd September, 1967) p1.

"LSD Girl says: I've Passed Truth Test" *Western Daily Press* (23rd September, 1967) p5.

Fletcher, Paul *Light upon the Path*. pp265, 270.

Greenfield, Robert *A Day in the Life: One Family, the Beautiful People, and the End of the Sixties*. Cambridge, US, Da Capo Press (2009) p116.

Pole, W.T. *Writing on the Ground*. London, Neville Spearman (1968) p51.

Pole, W.T. Letter to Rosamond Lehmann, dated 20th September, 1967 (original quoted courtesy of the Chalice Well Trust).

The Dragon Awakes

anon (W. Tudor Pole) "Preparing the Way for the New Age" in *Michael, Prince of Heaven* (1951) p30.

"Flower Group Probe Secrets of the Tor" *Bristol Evening Post* (18th September, 1967) p21.

"Flower People Seek 'The Truth' in Glastonbury" *Central Somerset Gazette* (22nd September, 1967) p1.

Hayes, Luther Newton *The Chinese Dragon*. Shanghai, Commercial Press (1922).

Michell, John "Lung Mei and the Dragon Paths of England" *Image* Vol. 7 No. 1 (Spring, 1968) pp17–24.

Michell, John Introduction to *The Sun and the Serpent*. p12.

Michell, John *The Flying Saucer Vision*. footnote pp147, 156–7.

Screeton, Paul *John Michell: From Atlantis to Avalon*. p19.

Two Merlins

Fenge, Gerry *The Two Worlds of Wellesley Tudor Pole*. pp155, 181.

Firth, Violet (Dion Fortune) *The Goat Foot God*. London, Williams & Norgate Ltd. (1936) pp88–9.

Fletcher, Paul *Light upon the Path*. pp86, 324.

Pole, W.T. *The Silent Road*. Glastonbury, Chalice Well Trust (1960) p223.

Screeton, Paul *John Michell: From Atlantis to Avalon*. p11.

Albina

"Glastonbury as Flying Saucer Centre Theory. Artist's Mural in New 'Temple'" *Central Somerset Gazette* (17th May, 1968) p1.

Michell, John "Lung Mei and the Dragon Paths of England" p24.

Michell, John Introduction to *The Sun and the Serpent*. pp13–4.

Latent Power in the Land

Levy, William "A Fortnight in the Life… On the Job in Swinging London" (2006 [1984]) online at: https://internationaltimes.it/a-fortnight-in-the-life-on-the-job-in-swinging-london

Michell, John "Centres and Lines of the Latent Power in Britain" *International Times* (19th October, 1967) p5.

Screeton, Paul *John Michell: From Atlantis to Avalon*. p19.

Confirmation in the Skies

"On the Air" *The Bookseller* (4th November, 1967) p23.

Green, Jonathon *Days in the Life*. London, Pimlico (1998) pp215–6.

Mathias, Michael and Walker, Brian "Flower Children Gather at Spiritual Centre of Britain: Hippies are Building their Heaven on Earth at Glastonbury"

Bristol Evening Post (4th November) pp16–7; cf 1st November, p1: "Here Come the Hippies".

Michell, John Introduction to *The Sun and the Serpent*. p12.

Peters, Pauline "Take me to your Saucer" *Sunday Times Magazine* (10th December, 1967) pp26–9.

CHAPTER THREE. *The Dragon in the Garden*

Embracing the Dragon

Michell, John "UFOs and the Message from the Past" *Albion* #1 (May, 1968) pp8–13.

Pole, W.T. *Writing on the Ground*. p99.

Gandalf's Garden

Caine, Mary "The Glastonbury Giants" in *Gandalf's Garden* #4 (March, 1969) pp16–21.

Leader, Elizabeth Letter in *Gandalf's Garden* #5 (1969) pp32–3.

Pepper, Jon "Glastonbury, the Hippies' Vale of Avalon" *Guardian* (20th December, 1969) p7.

Refinding Lost Knowledge

Critchlow, Keith "Introductory Notes on a New Theory of Proportion in Architecture with Particular Reference to Glastonbury Abbey" in Williams, Mary (ed): *Glastonbury: A Study in Patterns*. London, RILKO (1969) pp24–30.

Jackson, Janette "Glastonbury Abbey: The Ecclesia Vetusta" in Williams, Mary (ed): *Britain: A Study in Patterns*. London, RILKO (1969) pp47–52, 58.

Michell, John "Glastonbury Abbey: A Solar Instrument of Former Science" in Williams, Mary (ed) *Glastonbury: A Study in Patterns*. London, RILKO (1969) pp31–5.

Michell, John *The View over Atlantis*. London, Sphere Books (1972, second edition) pp34–5, 165, 189.

Information on RILKO (Research Into Lost Knowledge Organization) available online at: https://www.source watch.org/index.php/Research_Into_Lost_Knowledge_Organization

Russell, Geoffrey "The Secret of the Grail" in Williams, Mary (ed): *Glastonbury: A Study in Patterns*. London, RILKO (1969) pp16–9.

Twinch, Richard "Keith Critchlow: A Life Well Lived" (2020) online at: https://besharamagazine.org/remarkable-lives/keith-critchlow-a-life-well-lived/

Von Harten, Marjorie *Walking in the World*. Sherborne, Gloucestershire, Coombe Springs Press (1978) pp4–5.

Woolfe, Sam "How Geometric Hallucinations are Generated in the Brain" (2013) online at: https://www.samwoolfe.com/2013/06/a-model-of-how-geometric-hallucinations.html

Spaced Visitors

"The Crewe of Saucer Lines" *Central Somerset Gazette* (18th April, 1969) p8.

Faithfull, Marianne with Dalton, David *Faithfull: An Autobiography*. pp87–8.

Luckman, Michael *Alien Rock: The Rock 'n' Roll Extraterrestrial Connection*. New York, Pocket Books (2005) pp57–8.

Michell, John Introduction *The Sun and the Serpent*. pp13–4.

Miles, Barry *In the Sixties*. pp232–3.

"Vigil on Glastonbury Tor", picture caption in *Gandalf's Garden* #4 (March, 1969) p14.

Tolkien and the Garden

Bord, Colin "The Sacred Science of Antiquity" *Torc* #3 (February, 1972) pp14–6.

Carpenter, and Tolkien *The Letters of J.R.R. Tolkien*. pp306, 328.

Gandalf's Garden 'mission statement' – eg. issue #4, p2.

Hexham, Irving *Some Aspects of the Contemporary Search for an Alternative Society*. pp12, 18, 20, 29, 52 n9 & nn23–7, 57 n3.

Gandalf Broadcasting

Ashe, Geoffrey *King Arthur's Avalon*. p10.

Ashe, Geoffey "The Very Important Pilgrim" *Catholic Herald* (2nd July, 1965) online at: http://archive.catholicherald.co.uk/article/2nd-july-1965/3/the-very-important-pilgrim

Ashe, Geoffrey "Glastonbury: Key to the Future" *Gandalf's Garden* #4 (March, 1969) p15.

"Flower Power Hits the High Street" *Central Somerset Gazette* (20th June, 1969) p1.

"Hippies Move In" *Bristol Evening Post* (18th August, 1969) p4.

"Hippies use Healing Well for Washing" *Central Somerset Gazette* (22nd August, 1969) p1.

"Tor Fair is a Time to Remember" in the *Central Somerset Gazette* (5th Sept, 1969) p9.

Hexham, Irving *Some Aspects of the Contemporary Search for an Alternative Society*. pp5, 47 n9, 57 n3.

Lachman, Gary *Turn Off Your Mind: The Mystic Sixties and the Dark Side of the Age of Aquarius*. London, Sidgwick & Jackson (2001) p374.

Leyshon, Pat, Interviewed for 'Tracing the Map: Memorising Glastonbury High Street' (2001, part 3) online at: http://biggerhouseglastonburynetradio.blogspot.com/

Meiwana "Jesus and the Druids" in *Gandalf's Garden* #4 (Spring, 1969) pp14–5.

Miles, Barry *In the Sixties*. p232.

Oakley, Jan Interview with author (2024).

Pepper, Jon "Glastonbury, the Hippies' Vale of Avalon" p7.

Back to the Garden

Benham, Patrick *The Avalonians*. pp xvii–xviii.

Bickerstaffe, Scorpio. Interview with author (2024).

Deas, Francis Interview (2024).

Garrard, Bruce. Message to author (2024).

Mawson, Anthony. Message to author (2024).

Oakley, Jan. Interview with author (2024).

Pike, Rachel Interviewed for 'Tracing the Map: Memorising Glastonbury High Street' (2001, part 3) online at: http://biggerhouseglastonburynetradio.blogspot.com/

Shelly, John. Letter to Peter and Eileen Caddy (no date, possibly February, 1966). National Library of Scotland, MSS Findhorn Foundation, Acc.9934/24.

Shelly, John. Interviewed in "Look, Stranger" BBC2 (24th September, 1970) online at: https://www.youtube.com/watch?v=n8cAZaLhPjA

Town Hall Gigs: posters and commentary on the Facebook "Gbury Town then and now" page.

"Trip to the Truth" directed by Hugh Williams (first broadcast on BBC1, 10th January, 1972).

Fear of Ullage

"Hermit Group is told: Farm is not for Sale to you. Hippies Home Dream does a Fade-Out" *Western Daily Press* (11th December, 1967) p2.

"National Appeal on 'Hippies' Idea" *Wells Journal* (4th August, 1967) p1.

"Two are Found Guilty of Drug Charges. Opium Found in Car" *Central Somerset Gazette* (29th September, 1967) p3.

"No Camping on the Tor. Hippies cause Chalice Well Gardens Ban" *Central Somerset Gazette* (26th June, 1970) p1.

"Bulwarks Lane Development", cartoon caption *Central Somerset Gazette* (5th December, 1969) p3.

Well and Ill

Bickerstaffe, Scorpio, Interview with author (2024).

Deas, Francis, Interview with author (2024).

Pepper, Jon "Glastonbury, the Hippies' Vale of Avalon" p7.

Hexham, Irving *Some Aspects of the Contemporary Search for an Alternative Society*. pp6, 7, 11, 28–9, 48 n12, 50 n24, 58 n12.

"Hippies use Healing Well for Washing" *Central Somerset Gazette* (22nd August, 1969).

"Hippies may Move into the Town Car Parks" *Central Somerset Gazette* (26th March, 1971) p1.

"Dawn Raid to Move the Hippies" *Central Somerset Gazette* (19th March, 1971) p1.

Garrard, Bruce *Free State*. p12.

Stout, Adam *The Thorn and the Waters*. pp41–2.

Fletcher, Paul "The Story of the Guardians of Chalice Well. Part One: Taras and Moya Kosikowski" *The Chalice* #21 (Spring, 2008) pp10–4.

Fletcher, Paul *Light upon the Path*. pp73, 273, 318–22.

Pole, W.T. Letter to Rosamond Lehmann (dated 31st January, 1968, original quoted by courtesy of the Chalice Well Trust).

CHAPTER FOUR. *The First of the Festivals*

Class Players

Aubrey, Crispin & Shearlaw, John *Glastonbury: An Oral History of the Music, Mud and Magic*. London, Ebury Press (2004) pp30, 42.

Roberts, Andy *Albion Dreaming*. p157.

Hexham, Irving *Some Aspects of the Contemporary Search for an Alternative Society*, pp6, 22.

Kerr, Andrew *Intolerably Hip, passim*.

Spiritual Engineering

Baker, Phil "Making Albion Hum: John Michell Remembered" in *Fortean Times* (April, 2019) p45, pp46–52.

Critchlow, Keith, Detailed account of the building of the Pyramid Stage, based on Bill Harkin's account, taken down from the official festival website, which is frankly disturbing. Online (in French) at: https://www.glastotrip.org/histoire/chapitre-5-glastonbury-fayre/

Cunningham, John "Mystic Misfits" *Guardian* (22nd June, 1971).

Garrard, Bruce *Free State.* p14.

Kerr, Andrew *Intolerably Hip.* pp 197, 228, 232–4.

Michell, John *The View over Atlantis.* p192.

Michell, John "Lung Mei and the Dragon Paths of England", pp21–3.

Christing the Earth

Deas, Francis Interview with author (2024).

Cunningham, John "Mystic Misfits" *Guardian* (22nd June, 1971).

"Glastonbury Fair Manifesto" (a copy in Hexham: *Some Aspects*, Appendix 3).

Hexham, Irving *Some Aspects of the Contemporary Search for an Alternative Society.* p53 n19.

Kerr, Andrew *Intolerably Hip.* pp199, 224, 230, 233, 234, 326, 355, 356–7.

Roberts, Andy *Albion Dreaming.* p159.

Third Way Out

Ashe, Geoffrey *Camelot and the Dream of Albion*. London, Panther (1975) pp18–20.

Caine, Mary "Letters Between Mary Caine and John Maltwood".

Chapman, Christine, Interviewed in *Trip to the Truth*. BBC West (1972).

Ginsberg, Allen "The Art of Poetry" from interview in the *Paris Review* #37 (Spring, 1966).

Hexham, Irving *Some Aspects of the Contemporary Search for an Alternative Society*. pp20–2, 53 n16.

Loth, Wilfried *Building Europe: A History of European Unification*. Oldenburg, De Gruyter (2015) p157.

Meiwana "Jesus and the Druids" *Gandalf's Garden* #4 (Spring, 1969) pp14–5.

Michell, John "Centres and Lines of the Latent Power in Britain" *International Times* (19th October, 1967) p5.

Michell, John "Flying Saucers as a Portent of the Revelations which will Attend the opening of the Aquarian Age" *International Times* (30th Jan–12th February, 1967) p7.

Pole, W.T. *The Silent Road*. Glastonbury, Chalice Well Trust (1960) p223.

Shelly, John, interviewed in "Look, Stranger" BBC2 (24th September, 1970).

English Redemption Song

Eavis, Michael and Eavis, Emily, *Glastonbury 50*. London, Trapeze (2019) pp26–7, 188.

Kerr, Andrew *Intolerably Hip*, p228.

McKay, George *Glastonbury: A Very English Fair*. London, Victor Gollancz (2000) p21.

O'Connor, R. and Wilford, G. "Jeremy Corbyn at Glastonbury: Read Labour Leader's Pyramid Stage Speech in Full" *Independent* (25th June, 2017) online at: https://www.independent.co.uk/arts-entertainment/music/news/jeremy-corbyn-glastonbury-speech-read-full-pyramid-stage-crowd-size-a7806691.html

Priestley, J.B. "Britain and the Nuclear Bomb" *New Statesman* (2nd November, 1957) pp554–6.

Priestley, J.B. *English Journey*. London, Heinemann (1934) p143.

Roeg, Nicholas "Glastonbury Fayre", film released in 1972.

Young, Neil "After the Gold Rush", song released in 1970.

CHAPTER FIVE. *Madly Wrong or Madly Right?*

The Great Hippy Freak-Out

Vivienne Westwood and Malcolm McLaren "King's Road Royalty" online at: https://www.londonmuseum. org. uk/collections/london-stories/vivienne-westwood-malcolm-mclaren-kings-road-royalty/

Britton, Amy "Situationism Explained! And its Effect on Punk and Pop Culture" in *Louder than War* (20th July, 2012) online at: https://louderthanwar.com/situationism-explained-affect-punk-pop-culture/

End of the Line

Billingsley, John "Walking Myth into Place: Updating the Terrestrial Zodiac" from *Northern Earth* online article

(2024): https://northernearth.co.uk/walking-myth-into-place-updating-the-terrestrial-zodiac/

Michell, John "Lung Mei and the Dragon Paths of England".

Miller, Hamish and Broadhurst, Paul *The Sun and the Serpent* (1989).

Padavic-Callaghan, Karmela "Reality's Comeback" in *New Scientist* (7th September, 2024) pp32–35.

Screeton, Paul *John Michell: From Atlantis to Avalon.* Avebury, Alternative Albion (2010) pp19–20.

Stout, Adam *What's Real and What is Not: Reflections upon Archaeology and Earth Mysteries in Britain.* Frome, Runetree Press (2006).

Acid Archaeology
Roberts, Andy *Albion Dreaming,* pp204, 210–1.

www.ingramcontent.com/pod-product-compliance
Lightning Source LLC
Chambersburg PA
CBHW070808100426
42742CB00012B/2293